The Illusion of Parole

"Freedom is not a reality it's your lost birthright."

Boris I. Jones

www.fast-print.net/store.php

THE ILLUSION OF PAROLE

ISBN 978-184426-859-7

First published 2010 by
FASTPRINT PUBLISHING
Peterborough, England.

An environmentally friendly book printed and bound in England
by www.printondemand-worldwide.com

This book is made entirely of chain-of-custody materials

Dedicated to my best friend,
Pastor Edward Boskey,
also known as "Boochie"

Rest in Peace

Contents

"for you are still controlled by your sinful nature. You are jealous of one another and quarrel with each other. Doesn't that prove you are controlled by your sinful nature? Aren't you living like people of the world?"
(1 Corinthians 3:3)

Author's Last Words

I have always marched to the beat of a different drum and never felt like I have ever fitted in anywhere, nor have I ever tried. I have just always given myself to the thoughts and dreams that I am destined to do something special and then peacefully die without notice and all alone. All my life I believed in two things, one being my family which, I am sure when asked all will say the same about theirs, is the greatest in the world. The other is doing right by others, feeling somehow we are all connected and somehow directly linked to each other. I grew up all my life with a mother who made me feel like I could do anything; two sisters who always used to tell me God had plans for me; and two brothers who believed in me just the same and did things in their own special ways to keep me on track. My family is one that I would consider to be very religious or heavily involved in the Baptist or Christian faith, and although I grew up in the Baptist faith you might say I am the little lost black sheep of the family because I have been just the opposite. So opposite, I have lost sight or belief altogether in religious denominations and titles. Where they would go out and do God's works in the name of the church, and read their Bibles and attend their Bible Studies or retreats, me, I project my own beliefs in a far different place. Now a daddy myself with a beautiful wife, who happens to be Catholic, and four of the greatest children a man can ever dream of, I leave my Last Words for all to read.

"Now our knowledge is partial and incomplete, and even the gift of prophecy reveals only part of the whole picture! But when what is complete comes, then what is incomplete will be done away with." (1 Corinthians 13:9-10)

When I was a little boy I had many recurring dreams. However, there was one that reoccurred more than the others. I even continued to have it after I was grown and joined the military. It was simply a dream of me reading a book. Yes reading a book, something which I did not do very often. But me dreaming of reading a book is nothing special, only weird since it appeared to be the same book. Well, after so many years of dreaming of myself reading this book it was finally revealed to me why this dream was so special. One night in my dream I finally closed it and I was very surprised to see what secret the cover was hiding for so many years. For when I closed the book and saw the cover it left me with an image I would never forget. I felt very lost, but at the same time very surprised, for when I looked at the cover I saw what must have been the title but it was blurred and unreadable as if I was meant to focus on the next line and that one line alone. When I read the line in focus it simply said...

"Written By: Boris I. Jones"

Chapter One:
His Image, Your Soul, Our Universe "One Harmony"

"In the beginning was the Word, and the Word was with God, and the Word was God." (John 1:1)

My entire life I've always felt like I was alone even though I was always surrounded by loving family and friends. Yet still I could not escape an overwhelming feeling of being alone and depressed. I was also plagued with always having more questions than answers. I attempted to find these answers from many different sources, receiving no satisfaction. I always wondered how did we come to be, where did we really come from, is there more life out there beyond the skies of Earth? I have always wondered if and how it would be possible to travel to the far end of the galaxy and how the whole aging thing would work when doing so. There were so many questions that Ms. Salter nicknamed me

"Question". Ms. Salter was the little old lady who lived across the street from me when I was just a little kid living in Lincoln Shire, a small neighbourhood in Columbia, South Carolina. She used to love working out in her yard but it so happened she was terrified of earthworms. I remember the first time hearing her scream like she was under attack by monsters in a bad, black and white horror flick and, when I ran to her rescue, I was surprised to find one of Earth's giants standing over this small, white but ugly little worm screaming. She quickly ran to me and pleaded with me to get rid of it but, here is the kicker, she never wanted them harmed just simply relocated. And that was the beginning of a beautiful relationship. The little hero with the million questions who rescued the little old lady from the giant earthworms that were invading her space, the little old lady who attempted to answer him to the best of her abilities. Sometimes I think she called me over more for the attention and company than to slay the evil earthworm, since her loving husband had passed away, may he rest in peace. Nevertheless, it was a great match. I saved her from the worms and provided that ever-needed human contact, while she answered what must have added up to hundreds of thousands of questions over those years.

Well, needless to say, my questions continued and the answers, well, they were still noticeably absent. As I grew up I tried to find answers from friends, family, strangers, what some would call a secret society, that I found not so secret after all. But then again what is a secret if everyone knows? I even looked in the church. As a kid I did not really enjoy the church services all that well because all I could think about was, it's the weekend and I am here and I am sleepy. I experienced the same thoughts every Sunday until they would eventually fade out the Pastor speaking as I dozed off into sleepville. Later, I stopped going altogether.

I started school and found many answers, and I thought school was good, until I noticed none of the answers were to any of the questions I had. And when an attempt to answer one of my questions was made, even as a kid, I quickly smelt the answers for what they were. Life continued along with my problems of wetting the bed, nosebleeds day and night, sleepwalking inside and outside of my home, and problems with my breathing during the night. The problem was I would stop breathing for some unknown reason and run to my mother scared to death as she made me relax until my breathing restarted. I used to wonder why I was so different. Was I abducted by the little grey space guys or was I just crazy for thinking so? But just between you and me I actually thought I was abducted and had alien blood in me, at least that is what I used to tell people but, of course, no one paid me any attention.

Then I started having dreams that appeared a bit too real to be a dream, they was so vividly clear to the point that in one of them I could smell a chocolate cake that I saw on the table. I woke up from that fearing my dreams and thoughts because I knew there was more to life than what we can understand. I guess that is why I was always so fascinated with the Native Americans, the true founders and guardians of the land we now call the United States. Only it was not called the United States but to the natives it was known as the Land of the Creator. In all the shows I watched I noticed they had always recognized the Creator as the true owner of the land and, you know what, that sounds about right. I also believed that if anyone was connected to God it was them because of the way they live in harmony with the land. Don't get me wrong, I know there are a lot of cultures and races that live in harmony with the land and even demonstrate a very high level of intellect and working knowledge of the Universe, but still I found them to be the most appealing. I used to look at the movies and listen to the way they spoke, the way they lived by only taking from nature what was needed and not wasting anything, using every part of the slain animals for food, clothes and shelter while always giving credit to the Creator. I felt I learned more about God and the Spirits from them in the TV shows and movies than I learned from the education system and church. Sure, some would wonder how you learn so much from those stories which were being told from the other side, as they displayed their negative images and put the Indians in a negative light. I would simply tell you this, in every lie there's a hint of the truth, for the truth is the most powerful and a lie could never overtake the truth. The light will always displace the darkness and if your heart is open only to receive the lie, then the lie you shall receive and keep. If your heart is openly searching for truth then the truth will be revealed to you. However, my questions really started to grow as I saw show after show of mistreatment of the Native Americans and I wondered why they would treat the natives in such a manner. I thought to myself, how sad, and then I saw the film *The Diary of Anne Frank* and could not believe this was a true story. And then *Roots*, and images of Hitler and the Nazis, and those of Japan when they invaded China and my heart grew very heavy. It's like I took all this pain and suffering and stored it all inside and ever since I have lived in a sad and lonely depressed state. Don't get me wrong, I experienced great joys in life and even though my mother was forced to leave her home and run away from my father with her five kids she still managed to find a way to raise us all to be loving, caring and compassionate people who care about others sometimes more than ourselves. No matter how hard she had it she never wittingly let us see it. Although we grew up with much less than other kids in the refrigerator and cabinets she still managed to get us everything we wanted and needed for Christmas and our birthdays, and our kitchen was always open to our friends. But in seeing so much suffering my questions only grew in number and as I grew up and joined the military I again went to church to seek the answers to my questions but again felt disappointed. During my travels of the world I learned only of more pain and suffering, but instead of reading it from a book or seeing it on the television set I would be living right in the midst of it. I began to read the Bible, making the mistake of taking it at face value which only made me more confused. But my heart always felt things were not quite right and it was like the answers were staring me in the face all along.

So here I am 40 years later and finally I think I have found the answers to some of my most enduring questions. Of course, we will never have all the answers, for the truth of the matter is that our minds in the physical form would not be able to handle them. There are just so many answers of this nature we would be able to handle in this form, the rest we would have to receive in the spiritual form. Some will look at this as being a religious book and I will say to them it is not. It is neither fiction nor non-fiction, but simply my truths as I see them. Although this is not a religious book, I have learned one thing, you will never find any of the answers you seek if you don't come to one simple understanding. Get away from the names and titles because it is all linked, you will never know the truth without this simple understanding which is that what you call today's religion and history was once all in the same. Somewhere in the past someone decided that in order to separate and confuse the masses they would have to rewrite history and in the process separate any references to what is now called religion. Then they created an education system that does not include the religious aspects of the past, but instead a watered down version of what is needed to truly know our true selves. Then they sliced and diced what was to be the religion portion and then renamed the pieces to form separate religions with each group thinking they are the full truth. The small truth I have come to learn is that without learning your history as it was meant to be learned you will never understand the whys of today. The history you must learn is the entire history where State and religion are combined. You must understand that history, religion and today's News is all one and the same. In other words the three together will be tomorrow's history. Or another, more dramatic way of seeing it is as the future. And you will not know what is coming in the future without knowing religious aspects of history along with the rest of the history and paying close attention to today's News and the actual events taking place around you. The future is nothing more than history and religion repeating itself, only this time with different characters, better guns and more advanced technology. Although technology will continue to grow, the endless loop will continue until we all have finally found our own answers to the next three questions that I will simply word as: "His Image, Your Soul and Our Universe".

In my lost quest for answers, I now know there is no such thing when dealing with certain questions, but instead there are truths and untruths and everyone's truths may be of a different nature for as we are all different so will be each of our relationships with the Creators and the Universe. Still, the one true fact will remain, the Truth, no matter what the form, can only be the Truth. Here are my Truths as they relate to me and the Universe.

The Image of God

The Image of God, where do I start? I believe the Image of God is that of pure energy, consciousness, thoughts, intellect, and some other things that there has not been and will not be any words past, present or future of this planet nor any other planet, created or formed, to fully describe that which created and gave us life. I believe all of that will be revealed in the end days and then and only then will those who have been found worthy by the true Judge get to see God in his true form, learning to say his true name. So, from this point forward most of my references will be to the Creators, God and the Father. The Creators were there before the beginning of time, during our present times and long after our time has passed. They who have created us and all things that exist are eternal. They are so pure that all is created, achieved and performed, through thoughts turned to words which manifest into mass, matter and action. He was the sole being of which no word here or there will ever be created to describe his grandeur, which was so great that when he spoke his first word it was brought into being, and itself became a living being, and that which it named was brought into being, and it became a living being. The spoken word was "Light" and from that point forward the three co-existed in the deep darkness of space and water. Together they would create all that has been, that is and that ever will be.

Your Soul

"Beloved, now are we the sons of God, and it doth not yet appear what we shall be: but we know that, when he shall appear, we shall be like him; for we shall see him as he is." (1 John 3:2)

I believe that the Creators created Man in their true image and not that of the flesh but of the truest form, that of pure energy, consciousness, thought, intellect and that which is not known consciously to man.

"The Spirit gives life; the flesh counts for nothing. The words I have spoken to you are spirit and they are life." (John 6:63)

I believe this image of the Creators that we were blessed to posses is known to us as our version of the Soul, and I say "our version" because I also believe that all that lived, live and will live posses some form of a soul which is also held special to the Creators. This form of energy was the second to be spoken into existence by the Creators and the second to come into being. The first to become being was the "Word" which is the true Son of the Creators and together the Creators and the "Word" created "Light" in the Universe, making the original Light of the Universe the oldest living "Being" in existence. This is the true essence of the Creators themselves, that which no man has seen or will see until the end of days.

"And God said, Let there be light: and there was light." (Genesis 1:3)

After that the "Creator", which is the beginning and the end, the "Word" that was created from pure thought and intellect and the "Light" that was manifested by the Word into the purest form of energy was all that existed becoming the "Creators". I believe today that first Light is that which is known to us as the "Holy Spirit", the "Soul of the Universe". I believe that our Souls, which are located in our Minds, Thoughts, Intellect and very Conscience itself, hold all the secrets of the Universe. I believe our very souls are part of that which was created by the "Creator" in the beginning which was the "Light" and it's that which connects every being in the Universe to each other enabling us to live in harmony. This form of the Light that binds us is also known to us as "Love". However, "Man" was entrusted with not only the "Light" but the "Word" as well and the ability to create or manifest things into being through merely believing them into existence, leaving us as the caretakers of the great museum holding all the "Creator's" greatest masterpieces. Through the beliefs, faith, hope and love we were supposed to care for one another, the Universe and all there in it. As man evolved and grew more self-involved, the knowledge which we hold as secrets but is no more than common knowledge has been suppressed and buried. Buried under all our fatal tendencies such as hatred, idiocies, separations, racisms, untruths, arrogance, pride and greed that have somehow become the stone that blocks our path from eternal enlightenment.

Our Universe "One Harmony"

"In the beginning God created the heavens and the earth. And the earth was without form, and void; and darkness was upon the face of the deep. And the Spirit of God moved upon the face of the waters. And God said, Let there be light: and there was light." (Genesis 1:1–3)

In the beginning the Creators did not just create the Earth but instead they created something far greater. They created what we have come to know as the Universe, or "One Harmony" as I would like to think of it. I believe both scientists and religious scholars are right. The Universe as we know it was created by the "Big Bang". The big explosion, only it was not just any big bang but the thunderous roar of the Creator's voice, as it spoke the Word and the Word was "Light" and in an instance with great relevance it was so and that which was only darkness received balance and harmony with light that was created by the "Word" spoken by the "Creator". The darkness that covered the face of the deep was that vast darkness of space which was nothing like we have come to know it today, but that of space and water.

"And the earth was without form, and void; and darkness was upon the face of the deep. And the Spirit of God moved upon the face of the waters." (Genesis 1:2)

At this time there was no "One Harmony" but instead only the Creator himself until he spoke and said, 'Let there be Light,' and in an instant the first of what we would call explosions was created. Just as an atomic explosion at ground zero would create a blinding, brilliant flash of light and thermal waves of heat and energy so did this. But the brightness alone was brilliant and ripped through the void of space, darkness and water causing what must have been the greatest light show of all time that was trapped in a never-ending loop, since there was actually no "Time" at that time, forever ripping through the emptiness of space reflecting off the "Waters" through the darkness of the deep.

"God saw that the light was good." (Genesis 1:4)

This beauty could never be known to man in his human form but is still felt in his soul. This is why to this day we are all so fascinated with Space and the feeling of not being alone. When the Creators started the separations they separated the waters of Space by placing them in what we know as planets or Earth, but not just one Earth but many Earths. Just as the waters may be different types of water (liquids), so the Heavens (atmospheres) too would be of different types. Then on each of those Earths or Planets they separated the Heavens from the Waters. The planets consisting of different heavens, and different waters from those which are known here on Earth and each one arriving from their spoken word makes it that of the living.

"And God said, let there be a firmament in the midst of the waters, and let it divide the waters from the waters." (Genesis 1:6)

All that is living is one and that which was created by the Creators is living. All of his creations were brought into being in the same way by the same voice, with the same "Word", using the same "Light". The Creators can be found in all that was not created by the hands of "Man" but that which was created by those who are the "Alpha and the Omega", the "Beginning and the End". All things are living, "The Word and Light" being the eldest, followed by the day, night, time, planets, skies, dry ground on the planets, vegetation, sun, moon, stars, seasons, all the creatures of the seas, all the creatures with wings of every kind to fill the skies, all the living creatures of the land of every kind, and then in their image they created man.

"Male and female he created them." (Genesis 1:27)

We were created to be the caretakers of the Creators' glorious works of art to manage their property until their return.

"And God said, Let us make man in our image, after our likeness: and let them have dominion over the fish of the sea, and over the fowl of the air, and over the cattle, and over all the earth, and over every creeping thing that creepeth upon the earth." (Genesis 1:26)

Everything that was created was created in a specific order of the Creators' in order to build upon that which had been for the better. It is engraved in our very nature, in our souls to continue to build upon that which was created. This is why technology will always become more and more advanced, athletics records will always be broken, skyscrapers will get taller, planes will fly faster and higher, space shuttles will go further, generations will become smarter, and civilizations will continue to become more advanced, because we inherited the blessing to leave things better than we found them. Unfortunately, the blessing to continue to build upon that which already exists but with the original purpose of helping each other has become lost in man and in return the guns, bombs, wars and destruction of life continue to advance as well. As man and woman we should always be considering everything and everyone in every choice we make in life as we manage the Creators' creations with love and compassion for one another, living together in "Our Universe". And then, and only then, will we receive the full blessings of peace and enlightenment and for ever dwell in "One Harmony".

When you look at the Universe some may see it for just that instead of seeing it as one body that includes all living things within, to include the animals, the oceans, air, weather and space and time. Did you ever notice that sometimes your moods are affected directly by the weather? How, when it is cold, raining or foggy you seem to feel a little lonelier, sadder or depressed on those days while on the days where it is warm, hot and sunny you seem to be filled with much more energy? Well, this is not by chance. Since we were all created by light then, of course, we will get a bigger charge when there is more of it, but then you take away the light and it's time to sleep. Have you ever noticed that when a large part of the population's suffering is made known to you, you also feel a deep sadness fall upon you? Especially when it is a baby or child who is suffering, we get this overwhelming desire to want to ease their suffering. Well, we all feel this because we are all linked and the feeling is greater with a child because at birth the Spirit is strong in them because the child has not had the chance to dilute it yet with all the material factors of the world. The original light is the Spirit of the Creators themselves and the love is the Creators' spirit that is found within us all. And compassion is the light and love linking us all together causing the urge to cheer for others' success, and feel the warmth of their accomplishments, while at the same time causing us to feel sad, down and depressed in sight of their failures, pain and sufferings.

I often feel so linked with the world which is why I always had that feeling of being abducted even though I know I had not been. I truly lose strength and energy when there is so much negativity going on in the world. I feel so saddened by the needless killings and acts of violence we inflict on each other. The sadness I now know comes from knowing one truth. We will never know peace on earth until it is too late and we are in the days of the Judge. Light helps to create us, love helps to bond us, and compassion helps us to live connected in harmony. This in essence is what I believe when I hear the words, "His Image, Our Souls, One Universe", in short "One Harmony" as I would like to call it.

"This makes for harmony among the members, so that all the members care for each other." (1 Corinthians 12:25)

Chapter Two:
The Birthrights "Knowledge, Time and Destiny"

"But you have received the Holy Spirit, and he lives within you, so you don't need anyone to teach you what is true. For the Spirit teaches you everything you need to know, and what he teaches is true--it is not a lie. So just as he has taught you, remain in fellowship with Christ." (1 John 2:27)

In the beginning I had many questions and no answers, and the more I looked the less I found, because the more I looked the more I became lost. The more places I searched in the physical realm the further I went away from the spiritual realm to find that which I sought. I had first to know where to look, but I never thought to look to the one place where, in the end, the answers would be found - within me. I have always felt things and read things but I thought it cannot be. And the more I thought with that of the physical mindset the further I pushed my answers away. You know gravity exist on

Earth, and you know there is none in Space. And you know this because you have read it and been taught that in Space there is none and there is less on the Moon. But then one day you visit the Moon and your rations for the entire trip sit on a pallet and you want to move it. Even though you feel the lesser pull of gravity on your body, still your mind thinks, when I lift I needed to lift hard because the pallet was going to be heavy. But when you do so, you throw your life rations into Deep Space. Now you felt the lesser gravity and you were taught about the lesser gravity but still you will go hungry because you did not trust what you felt. Now, you may survive one day, or even three, but one day you will surely die because of the lack of rations. Sometimes you just have to trust what you feel because what you are feeling from within comes from the source and the source knows nothing but truth because lies are not of it. I say all that to tell you this, I am not trying to teach you anything with these words, even if I continue to write till there is a compilation of a thousand pages there will be only one underlying truth, what you seek is within you and only you. I am only sharing my truths with you.

There are a lot of organizations, secret societies, government agencies both foreign and domestic, and churches all over the world, even the crazy people, and dishonest people, and the list goes on and on of those who claim they know, hold, protect and guard the true secrets of life, salvation, the Universe and the human soul. They claim they are keeping it from you to protect you, and from whom do they protect you? Is it God the creator of all things? NO. Is it the devil the destroyer of all things? NO. And if not them then who, and why do they feel they need to protect us from something we all have inherited since the beginning of the existence of life itself? The knowledge they claim they hold is nothing compared to the common knowledge we all inherit at birth, but lose in the great conspiracies, cover-ups, hoodwinks, wool-overs, brainwashings, religious movements, education systems, self-arrogance and the great Corporation schemes of corruptions. The truth of the matter is they are protecting themselves.

Since his creation, man has felt the power and craved more ever since. Every rule, law, bill, theory, religious scroll, play script, constitution, declaration, secret manuscript, charter, contract, by-law, News article, television and movie script, book report, love note, was written with one thing in mind and one thing in common… to give "Man" power, control and authority over another. Understand this, the only secret worth seeking is that which you possess in your own mind and soul, and even that will be lost to you if you do not open your heart and soul for understanding. You can solve most of your issues and problems by simply asking yourself a few questions, but when asking you need to ensure you are doing so with every intention of receiving an answer back. All truths are inside you, you have the power and or ability to do and be anything you want.

I remember a time when I was deep into making music, but in the beginning I did not have a clue as to how to make music, never mind even hook up the equipment. I tried so hard to get all this equipment to work so I could try to make my own music, just as my brother Stan did before me, but to no end. I could not get it to work. I remember thinking, I have all this junk and I don't have a working knowledge of how to use it. Then one night I went to sleep and in my dream I saw myself in my home studio and I was hooking up this equipment as if I'd just graduated from some form of schooling on this type of equipment. But it was not the speed and efficiency I possessed when I was hooking up this equipment I was seeing, but it was the clothes that I was wearing. White baggy shorts I had cut from my favourite pair of pants after they had gotten too short. They were white shorts covered all over with cartoons without the colours, just the black outlines of the drawing. This really caught my attention because it was those white shorts and black T-shirt that I had decided to wear to bed that night. What else caught my attention was the way everything was positioned in the room, which was the way I had left it prior to going to bed that night. What was so odd about this dream and unlike the others was it was like I was in the room watching myself hook up this equipment as if I had certain knowledge of hooking up the equipment to make it work. You can imagine that I felt somewhat lost to know that I was asleep, and knew I was asleep, but at the same time felt wide awake and in the studio. Here is the really crazy part, I felt like I was awake in the dream working on the equipment and awake in the room watching myself hook up the equipment while at the same time I knew very well that I was asleep in my bed. I wanted to wake up but, knowing what I was doing, I stayed asleep as I carefully watched myself hook up each and every piece of equipment. And as soon as I finished hooking up the equipment I turned it all on to run some tests and it worked. This is when I woke up in the night and went into my studio and when I turned on the light that is when I saw it. The room was exactly as I left it before going to sleep and exactly as it had appeared in my dream. So I began to retrace my steps as I had watched with two set of eyes, one from where I was watching myself in the dream, and the other watching myself from outside of the dream. I went step by step without having to think of what to do, but only to remember what I did in the vision. When I was done I went to test the system and, lo and behold, not only did it work, but I knew what tests to do to check it, and had working knowledge of how to operate it as well. Now most will not believe this story but then it will be many who believe it wholeheartedly because they have, in fact, had the same type of experience. I trusted that which I learned in the spiritual realm to the effect that the knowledge which I did not know in the physical realm became known.

All that is fine and all that, but here are the questions that still screw with my mind after all these years. When I went to sleep that night it was two of me in the dream, one that was hooking up the equipment and one that was watching from within the dream. Then it was me who was actually dreaming and watching from the outside as with a normal dream. My question is who, why, where or when were the three individuals? Had I actually travelled to the future, watching my future self? And if my future self was the one who was actually doing the work, who was the me that was watching them from within the dream? Was it the past me who had seen me in the dream, which would have made the me on the outside dreaming and seeing the two from the outside the present me? The bigger question is how did the future me have working knowledge of the equipment if, in fact, the past or present me did not? Then I realize and remember what was revealed to me, there is no order and structure of time in the spiritual realm. There space-time is one and is without order. All there is, is that which is, and in this case that which was, was the working knowledge of the equipment.

"But you have an anointing from the Holy One, and all of you know the truth." (1 John 2:20)

Although destiny is something you have no control over, still it is something you can control greatly. Yes, I know that sounds a bit contradictory but to understand that you need to understand space and time. You need to understand that life in the human form and that of the spiritual realm are far different in comparison. Time does not travel in straight lines as most of us are led to believe with our organized calendars and planned-out events. Am I saying just forget time as we know it? Yes and no. In the flesh or physical realm I am certainly not, it adds structure to our life. Even when the Creators created all that of the physical realm they did it within the bounds of time. In fact, the moment they started to create the physical realm, time started. They created all that we know in the first seven days of time existence. So what am I referring to when I say time is not structured or does not travel in a straight, neat and organized fashion, except for when we're in the physical realm? Well, I will tell you. I am saying time is boundless and endless. In the beginning, time was just there to relate it to the physical world. Imagine having a clock just before time began and that clock was linked to time itself. Well, when you looked at that clock the hands never moved, and the hands stayed still for there was no time, until the Creators said let there be Light, and in that moment the hands on the clock began to move. That was the moment time came into existence. Yes, time is also bounded by that of the living as is the air, wind, water, fire and earth.

Once time enters the physical realm it becomes structured, it becomes victim to the boundaries which were placed upon the physical realm by the Creators. The Creators set the structure of time when they named the light "Day" and the dark "Night" because that very evening and morning became the first day (Genesis 1:5). This means they started the clock once the creation of the physical realm began. That's in the physical realm, outside of the physical realm time has no boundaries, control nor structure, it returns to its original state where the hands on the clock stop moving. All of these words I am writing require neither proof nor scientist to verify, all you have to do is look within yourself for the answers as with all the answers you may need or be in search of. Here is a simple way to test this logic that requires very little time and effort. Just close your eyes and see if you can travel back in time, or anywhere in the present, and even the future which takes much more focus and concentration but should be possible. You may call them memories which are boundaries bestowed upon you by man and the education system when in fact it is your inner being, your conscience travelling through the spiritual world in a time that is free of boundaries and structure. If that does not work for you then here is a more physical test which logically should work. Close all the windows in your room, seal off the ability of all the outside light to get in. Unplug all the clocks and remove all the watches from the room as well and you will find that with no knowledge of the physical time, your internal clock will grow very slow, and then extremely slow, and what we know as a 24-hour clock will begin to change greatly in hours, becoming 28, 30, 36, 40 hours in length. You will find yourself actually sleeping less and staying awake longer with no visible effects. I can say this for certain after experiencing this in a lesser situation. Nevertheless, my time as I knew it changed. My eating habits, rest room cycles and sleep cycles all changed. I was going longer on less. If you talk to your friends and neighbours I am sure you will find that someone you know, if not you yourself, has experienced this already.

Now, getting back to the second chapter of my book before I completely write the third, how does this knowledge affect your destiny? Well, your destiny in the physical realm is already predestined and is set in motion and appears to be unchangeable which is true in the physical realm. But in the spiritual realm, time and destiny have no structure. Which is why the Bible speaks of having faith the size of a mustard seed will give you the ability to move mountains. It's telling you that you must believe, focus and concentrate all of your mental thoughts on believing the change you want to make. When you focus, concentrate, believe, and I mean truly believe or in a word pray, you are joining the Creators in the spiritual realm, removing your boundaries set in the physical realm by man and God. Why else would a man or woman who truly believes with all their heart as a child that they would grow up to be an athletic star, movie star, or music star grow up to accomplish just that? You can say, 'What about the ones who did not make it?' Well, you must look at each individual on an individual basis but, as a whole, that remains the case.

Let's take my life which you will hear about all through this book since it is that which this book is founded upon. When I was a child barely able to walk I said I would grow up to be a soldier and serve in the army. I knew with all my heart I was going to be a soldier, I never deviated from that thought or had dreams of being anything but. Even as I grew and realized I had other skills and talents, still the one thing I knew above all else was I was going to be a soldier. As I was growing up I saw in dreams the place I was going to be stationed. I knew where I would go first with great certainty without ever visiting the place. The place I am speaking of was Germany. I saw in my mind that I was going to be a soldier and specifically knew the place I would be stationed so much till, as a kid, I started having what appeared to me were dreams at the time but I later came to find out that in fact they were not dreams but, as the wise Native American Indians called it, visions. I did not know this until later.

I grew up and I joined the army and my first duty station was Germany, and while there I had many very bad cases of *déjà vu*. I was going places where I just knew I had been or seen before. How could this be because I know for certain I had never been to this country at any point in my life? The individuals I was with during some of those moments used to ask me what was the matter and I told them I felt like I had been to those places before. And this was when I first heard the expression *déjà vu* related to myself, because that is what one of my friends told me I was experiencing. One day, I was seeing this place in my mind as if I had been to it before, but because I knew it could not be I dismissed it. But later that night in my mind I was seeing myself going to the location by what appeared to be bike or foot because I was going through the woods, passing trees and then through beautiful open fields until I saw this church or cathedral tower with a large clock on the face. And then I realized this was too real to still be a dream because even when I woke up I was still able to recall it very vividly. The next day I went to one of my friends and borrowed his bike for the day and I took off. In what direction to travel I did not know so I started by riding out of the front gate of the military installation nicknamed "The Rock", which was a small army base I was living on, and I just continued to go. I remember it being so peaceful on that bike riding in the countryside of Kirsch Geon's Germany until I came upon a familiar sight that mesmerized me. I came out in a little town, riding towards what appeared to be a church or small cathedral with a clock on the face. Only this was not just any church or cathedral with a clock on the face of it but it was the same church or cathedral with the clock on the face of the tower from my dreams growing up and that previous night in my dreams. It was so vivid that I can still remember the time on the clock till this day. The time was 15:45 in all my dreams, and I know this because I always thought the clock of that church or cathedral must have been broken because every time I saw it, it was the same. The same, that is, until I came across it in person. The time, if you had not guessed it by now, was 15:45; I sat and stared at the clock as the hand changed to 15:46, 15:47 and I thought to myself, is this really happening? So I began riding the bike following the same route as in my dreams and there it was, the small club I had visited a few times in my dreams. After all these years the name escapes me, but even unto now I am urged to say the name that continues to come with the dream but will not. In that moment I realized something special had happened, and after a 21-year military career I am here to say our destinies are ours to set or change, only the process is done in the spiritual realm. We all are born with the ability to set or change our destiny with a great deal of pure intellect and knowledge, along with the ability to move freely through space-time.

Unfortunately, as in all stories, there are always villains and in this story there is no difference. There are great works being undertaken by these villains who from this point will be known as the "Corporation". Their intentions are to imprison every living soul on this planet and the next, in an invisible prison without any physical restraints, stripping away your birthright which is all knowledge which every child inherits at birth with their soul from the Creators. Their only desire is to grow in power and to rule over not only all the physical beings created by the Creators but the very "Soul" of the Universe itself. It's time you remember, for the truth is within you and the end shall come for it has been written in the Book of Life and that which has been written will surely come to pass. Now is the time for now we are in the last days and the end will arrive very fast without warning.

"See that what you have heard from the beginning remains in you. If it does, you also will remain in the Son and in the Father." (1 John 2:24)

Chapter Three:
Entering the Great Courtroom

When looking at the world, it's time you saw it for what it really is, which is nothing more than a courtroom. And if I may, I would even call it the 'Great Courtroom' for none is greater. Its walls are the very edge of the Universe itself which borders neither here nor there but everywhere, also known as the spiritual realm. Innocent until proven guilty carries a far greater meaning in the grand scheme of today's reality in this physical and spiritual courtroom. It does not just mean you are a suspect in a crime known and committed in the world of Man but also in a trial that carries on to the spiritual realm as well. From the time of conception until entering the Great Courtroom in most cases nine months will pass. During that time you have been touched and comforted by those with no name, learned the truest form of love which is to love without conditions intertwined in compassion. You learned the knowledge of the Universe from those of endless knowledge and limitless intelligence; you've been given the intellect and ability to set your own destiny, and the know-how of travelling through space-time. You've visited every corner of the Universe and all that is in between them and experienced a union and dwelled in the presence with all of the Creators' creations from the distance Earths. You've received gifts and souvenirs from the Father himself to hold and cherish throughout your lifetime. These gifts and souvenirs manifest themselves throughout your life in your athletics skills, your imaginative creativity, unsurpassable levels of intellect, the extraordinary linguistic abilities, prophesy, healing abilities, and the ability to read minds. The list goes on and on with things such as: breathing fire; holding your breath above average times; walking on nails, fire and glass; metal piercing the flesh without pain; being fearless; extra lives; ability to speak to and understand animals; visions, etc. All of this is a gift of love from love itself, but in the physical realm it's a violation of "The Corporation's Laws of Orders" which are maintained out of chaos. Since we all inherit one or more of these gifts and or souvenirs at birth we are instant suspects and monitored until these special traits are either erased or wiped from our memories in the physical realm or put to use by the Corporation.

"Who is the liar? It is the man who denies that Jesus is the Christ. Such a man is the antichrist--he denies the Father and the Son." (1 John 2:22)

The true secrets of the Universe in themselves are the secrets of the Corporation and their motives and intentions and the underlying truth behind it all, which is to keep you from knowing the truth. As you journey forward through your trials the secrets will be revealed only to be dismissed by each of you, or worse, accepted in exchange for a seat with the Corporation. While going through your trials in the Great Courtroom your only defence will be "The Living Truth" in its purest form, because "The TRUTH, The Whole Truth, and Nothing but the Truth SHALL SET YOU FREE." To find that which you seek, you need only to look within yourself, for the knowledge you seek is kept by no man but God himself in trust in the spiritual realm for all the children of Adam and Eve, who first received the knowledge by partaking of the forbidden tree of knowledge, to inherit for all eternity. While in trust it will draw interest which will result in each generation growing smarter than the previous and the trust is kept in the spiritual realm and released only by the Holy Spirit, to the Spirit or Soul of each individual at birth. Look at it this way, as man being an analogue tape; the more you record onto the tape the more the data is degraded. Then look at the Holy Spirit and your Soul or Spirit as being a digital hard drive and you can copy the data from one digital source to another a million times and it will remain the same. If this knowledge was passed from Adam and Eve in the physical or analogue way it would have been degraded and corrupted by the end of the first generation. As evidence of the analogue word, the Bible was changed and degraded. Instead, the knowledge is retrieved after every death by the Spirit and passed to every spirit during birth, ensuring the knowledge not only remains but grows over time with nothing lost. In the end the pure digital knowledge of the Spirit will help you decode the old antiquated analogue knowledge of man.

"I do not write to you because you do not know the truth, but because you do know it and because no lie comes from the truth." (1 John 2:21)

Chapter Four:
A New Birth; A New Trial

"God blessed them and said to them, "Be fruitful and increase in number; fill the earth and subdue it. Rule over the fish of the sea and the birds of the air and over every living creature that moves on the ground." (Genesis 1:26)

When a child is born into today's society, automatically he is already immersed in a trial that will determine where he is placed in society. And although there are different levels in society, in most cases the child will be found guilty and sentenced to life in the Great Prison Without Walls. How can we have a prison without walls, some may ask, and it is this I will say, since it is not your human or physical state that is being imprisoned then no physical barriers of any sort are needed. Since it is actually your spiritual state being imprisoned then the walls to the prison can be that of a spiritual nature as well. Why must our true nature be imprisoned is the question, and how can we be set free? The reasons are obvious and well known, because they are the age-old reasons which consist of power and greed. Since the beginning of time, battles have been waged for power over the souls of the world. Each child has the ability to be born with special gifts from the Lord and that is something the Corporation will not allow to happen if they have their way, so they work really hard to stop your true nature from manifesting. The thing they know better than anyone is that history and religion are sure to repeat themselves, and although they cannot stop the return of the Saviour they will do whatever it takes to try, even prolonging it if they have to.The Corporation is not completely starting the process any more, in fact they have things set on auto now and it is actually we, the parents, who are starting the process and determining the fate of our children. Most of us have been encoded and imprisoned so long they have us institutionalized and we don't even know it. So we begin to pass down the triggers to our children which is sure to set them on the wrong paths from the start. Some things are out of our control but for the most part there are things we can do to start our children on the right journey. For starters, your good or bad habits in life will surely be passed on to your kids in some way or form. If you are the type of person who is doing drugs, drinking or abusing the mother you are hurting your child. If you are that racist, hateful, ignorant individual then you are hurting everyone. When a child is born he is born innocent and pure but bearing the sins of all who came before him. We should love our children and set them up for success no matter the cost to ourselves, because it is in our nature to build upon what is already there. When a baby is born his mind is like a sponge and between birth and four years old your child stands to learn the highest percentage of his lifetime's knowledge. His value system will start to be developed. There is no need to teach your child how to love, because a child is born of unconditional love, mercy and compassion and it is in a child to love without thought and or conditions because all spirits or souls come from the Creators and God is Love. We as parents will either nourish that love or we will turn that love to hate.

"The Spirit gives life; the flesh counts for nothing. The words I have spoken to you are spirit and they are life." (John 6:63)

We should encourage our children's growth and help them to develop their gifts from the Universe, and the Creator himself. Racism helps no one but it hurts everyone and it continues a cycle that needs to be broken, and it starts with the way each of us develop our children. Instead of passing our hate to our children we should encourage them to dream and utilize their imaginations as much as possible, as well as considering what they would like to be at an early stage in their life and then put the mechanisms in place to provide them assistance and encouragement to accomplish their dreams. It's time we began to teach our children about the different religions of the world, but not as the enemy, but a different part of the whole. It's time that they learned that Islam, Judaism, Buddhism, Hinduism, Baha'i, Christianity, Confucianism, Jainism, Judaism, Shinto, Sikhism, Taoism, Wicca, Zoroastrianism, and Druidism etc. are all part of the body of the Creators. They are merely part of the whole because no one religion is the whole. It would be like calling your leg or arm your body, and in order to get along we must understand and respect each other's differences. We must teach them that one may not respect the other from ignorance but it's up to the others who know better to protect the ones who are lost, and not hate or try to change them. We must teach them that any religion that recognizes that Jesus is the son of God, the Word which was sent in the flesh to teach us and show us that God's word was not impossible and that life in the flesh can be lived without sin, regardless of the forces surrounding us, is of the body. Those who speak against the Son love not the Father and their words are a lie and they are not of the body of Christ.

"The body is a unit, though it is made up of many parts; and though all its parts are many, they form one body. So it is with Christ." (1 Corinthians 12:12)

Today's society is set up to strip your children of their greatest gifts which are: their imagination, which is linked directly to their creativity; their ability to love indiscriminately and unconditionally; and their birthright, which is their link directly to the Universe. The system was set in place to get both parents out of the home and into the workforce so as to have better control over what goes into the heart and mind of every child. Now, instead of at least one of the parents maintaining direct control of the child's learning and growth they are carted off to school for further manipulation and brainwashing. You take the educations system and mix it in with all the negative images posted on the walls, television, movies, video games, News and Internet and you have yourself one great big human manipulation machine. Leaving your child's spiritual inner being to be constantly tested, tempted and tried. Before they even reach the age of ten there are marketing campaigns created with the sole purpose of drawing their future business which leads to even more degradation of their inner beings. The Corporation wants your children to be focused on the televisions, video games, music and computers in order to strip away their imaginations and slow their ability to learn and grow. To raise their hate levels for their brothers and sisters of the world, stripping away their abilities to love each other as the Father commanded. When it is all said and done they want a society of obedient, mindless slaves while they suck all the money out of the world and make the masses have to depend on them for everything. In the end what they want is to rule the "WORLD" and they know the true secret. The future of the planet will be determined by the minds and hearts of the children. No one said it better than the great Mrs. Whitney Houston as she so perfectly stated, 'Don't you know the children are the future?' This is a statement that holds more truth than most people know. Now is the time to protect those who will determine the fate of the world. It's time to defend our children as they go through their trials of life and injustices of the world, arm your children with the greatest weapon you can give them. Start by arming them with their imagination: read to them instead of letting them live in front of the television; buy the simple toys and building blocks instead of the video games; teach them that all life is precious and that all nationalities and religions are part of the whole. Teach them not to get caught up in the name brands, titles, medals, awards and trophies, by placing these things above the love of the game. Encourage their creative good behaviour and respectfulness with awards and discipline, or correct their lazy, bad attitudes, rudeness and disrespectful ways immediately. Teach them of the Creators and that the Spirit of the Creators resides within them, and that Jesus was the Word that manifested in the flesh and died for their sins. Teach them he showed his love by walking the world knowing he would die a brutal death. He did it in order to teach and show us all unconditional love, compassion, empathy, sympathy, mercy and, most of all, forgiveness, as he so gracefully walked by faith and not by sight. After you have done all of this and given your children a nice foundation of well fertilized soil, then and only then it's okay to allow some of the materials of the world to be used, for they will not overtake the seeds you have planted in the light.

Chapter Five:
The First Dream "The Defendant Opening Statement"

"Honour your father and your mother, as the LORD your God has commanded you, so that you may live long and that it may go well with you in the land the LORD your God is giving you." (Deuteronomy 5:16)

During your lifetime you will have many individuals representing you and defending you as you travel on the path that destiny has laid for you. All of these individuals will have a direct impact on the outcome of your life, both in the physical realm and the spiritual realm as well. But there are two who will reign true above all the rest and, although there may be substitutes for them, in the grand scheme of things they are the most natural defenders. Who are they? Well, that is easy, they are your parents, and they will be the ones who will give your opening statement.

Now the opening statement they give will be highly critical in the future development of the defendant. If they give a negative opening statement then this will surely affect their child's ability to learn and grow. For instance, if the opening statement that goes on record is filled with comments such as: you will never amount to anything; you are so lazy you are going to be just like your no-good daddy (or momma); you are about useless, you don't have brain in that head of yours, then these statements will either motivate your child to succeed or, in most cases, they will have a negative impact on the child's psyche and surely he will grow into the role that idiot parent had set for him. During his trial he or she will surely be found guilty in the Great Courtroom and sentenced to a life of insecurities, low self-esteem and a lack of confidence in themselves. If they give an empty opening statement of very little or no substance then, just merely by omission of the positives or negatives, they will leave the child in limbo trying to please or live up to standards he or she may have already passed. But because it was unknown, the child was left feeling as if he or she was not good enough or, even worse, that the task is too great.

However, when the defender goes on the record with an opening statement that is passionate and full of substance with positive comments such as: God has great plans for you; oh, he is so smart he will be whatever he sets his mind to; baby, you can be anything you want; daddy and mommy are so proud of you; oh, what a blessing you are; what a great job you have done; and the number one positive of all, I love you baby, then these statements will surely impact your child's future in a manner such as to elevate them to a whole new level that will surely affect the outcome of their life trials in a very positive way. The defender will provide the nourishment and first line knowledge to the child.

I grew up without my father and at some points in my life it left me without many of the things the other little kids had, such as that male father figure to look up to and to teach me things, and at times without some provisions that other little kids had. However, what I did have was four other siblings and one of the greatest defenders the Universe had to offer, and between the five of them they gave an opening statement for me that was not to be undone. My mother, a single lady left to raise five little kids on her own ranging from the ages of two to eight years, not only gave some of the most powerful opening statements any defender could have given but she delivered them brilliantly. Even during the time when she was suffering having to leave a marriage that had some major issues. Even though she was forced to leave with nothing, having no home, no car, no money, no food, no clothes and no ideas, she had to swallow her pride and take her five kids to her sister's home (may she rest in peace) and ask if we all could stay with her until she could get on her feet. Now, that was not just her sister but Mrs. Thelma Dawson, better known to us as Aunt Pug who was not only another single woman but one who did not play. She was a hard woman but fair. She was a great cook also, but most importantly she was my friend and my favourite aunt, who was also raising five kids alone in a three-bedroom apartment in the projects. Of course, my Aunt Pug said yes and there we all were, 12 people living in a three-bedroom apartment in the projects with two families trying to co-exist, and that we did. But not because we had everything, but because we had the greatest defender the Universe had to offer, my mom Mrs. Elizabeth Jones. Though she was at her worst moments in time she still found the courage and the strength to deliver such impressive opening statements as: 'you all will be something'; 'I will do whatever it takes to get us our own home with a big front and back yard'; 'my baby is so smart he can do anything'; 'you should know better than that'; 'you are smarter than that and should know better'; 'baby fix momma's fan or fix momma's clock radio - but I can't - yes you can, momma knows you can'; 'I love you'; 'praise the Lord'; 'Momma's sorry baby, but don't worry'; and her number one statement, 'God have mercy'. Through the worst times of her life when she was at rock bottom trying to figure out how she would even feed her kids, she still managed to deliver opening statements so powerful that all five of her kids came out of the situation untarnished and unblemished by the fact we went without a father and any assistance from him with the exception of the *one* child support payment he made to her of a hundred dollars. Never did she talk down about him, nor ever try to stop us from seeing him. We, like many other children in the world, were left with only one defender and I praise the Creators for such a choice. I certainly credit much of our success to her opening statements, her examples of strength and courage in the face of adversity.

I also still give a little credit to my father for, whatever the reasons, he decided to stay away and did not make any trouble for us. Now does he deserve credit in many ways? He does because I told myself I would never be my father and although what he did was a negative I took it and made it a positive. Does he deserve resentment for what he did? Who knows? That is between him, my mother and the true Judge, for I am only a son who did not have the honour of growing up with my father. But let it be known, if the opportunity existed today I would take it in a heartbeat. Well, in any case, it's too late now for the chance to be loved by my father in the physical realm but not too late to love him in both the physical and spiritual realm. So I have self-appointed myself as his attorney, or just maybe he had reached out and appointed me himself for I used to have the weirdest dreams. I used to always see my father in my dreams standing under a pecan tree. I never knew the meaning of this dream, I did not know if it was a dream or just a memory until one day a couple of years back me and my brother sat in the car at the DMV and my brother revealed to me some shocking news. All my life I thought my father died in an accident he had at work, but on this day in the car my big brother revealed to me that it was not the case. My big brother had learned from our grandfather that our daddy had not died in a working accident but instead had been murdered. He told me that our father had been killed and left under a pecan tree. And just as he had lived so did he die, all alone with no family or friends to his side, just an old pecan tree which linked him to his baby boy. I was never given the chance to properly mourn my father's death so now, after his death, his baby boy is his defender and for him my opening statement will simply be, 'I love you daddy', and 'I forgive you will all my heart', and to borrow a great opening statement from my defender I add, 'Lord please have mercy on him for he is my father and as you love your Son and he loves you so do I love my father. I call on your promise of love and compassion, and your promise to have mercy on those who love your Son and ask for things through him. So in

Jesus' name I pray you find room at your great table and allow my father a seat so he may eat well for now and all eternity'.

My father may not have been present but still I found opening statements in the words and the actions of my two brothers and two sisters. My sister Melissa, the eldest of the five, was also a great source of strength and admiration. In my eyes she could do no wrong even when she was dragging my little spoiled butt through the house by my legs when I was crying too much. She is going to kill me for writing that but in any case she was and is the greatest. I don't think there was ever a time I did not look up to my big sister. I was always so proud of her when she went off to college on her own. She was the only one of us to go away and graduate out of college. I was so proud when we went to her graduation, she had always been one of my greatest defenders which drove me to want to have that very freedom and independence of living on my own. It always seems as if she knew what she wanted and was not afraid to go get it. As my defender she had always been proud of me, and always been the first to tell me how proud of me she was. She would always talk about her little brother to her friends. I even think she may have bored some poor strangers as well but in any case I have always felt extremely special as a result of her pride in me. I always placed it off when she spoke of such things but little did she know I always left her with tears in my eyes. Every time she would try to hug and kiss me I would just take off running. Even until now, though I am 40 years old, she is still talking about her little brother with such great pride, and still trying to hug and kiss me and, yep, you may have guessed it, I am still running, only to shed my tears in private as I always feel such sadness when I am driving away.

My big sister is no stranger to the economic downfalls caused by the Corporation. In fact she has gotten caught up in the economic downfalls several times but, somehow, she has always managed to keep her faith and her head up. Just as our mother did during her trying times, my big sister still somehow finds time to send encouragement to me and others. She has always found her way back and still keeps her faith. Currently, she has once again became a victim of the Corporation's intentional shifts of the world economies leaving her unemployed once more. Yet she still manages to be a source of strength for me to draw upon, as she still finds time to show excitement in dealing with me wanting to write a book. I just say to her that all things happen for a reason, just as she and my sister Debbie have told me many times. And it's time I sent this message back to her, worry not for this is all in the plans that God has for you. Just stay on point and things will become clear very soon.

My other defender may have delivered one of the biggest boosts to my life as well, which is my other sister Debbie. She has been with the same man, who is my big brother John, for over 30 years. She has been a great example of God's love, and while that is great it is not what brings her to my trials as one of my defenders. What makes her part of my defender team is her spiritual gifts. My sister has travelled to the realm of the spirits and back, has spoken in tongues where the only one who could understand her was God himself, and she always had a message for me, and the message was always short and simple, but a very powerful statement. The message was, 'Bob, God has plans for you'. She told me this every time she saw me as I was growing up and now many years later I finally get it. It may be the shortest of the stories about my defenders but I assure you it was absolutely one of the most powerful.

These are the individuals who delivered their opening statements for me by their very words. However, the next three delivered theirs by their actions. First being my oldest brother Leamon. His actions have always been those of a silent nature. Even though he has been blessed with the gift of the gab and the ability to make you laugh or cry with his very words, it has always been his actions that brought me the greatest pride and honour of being his little brother. It may take me a day to write a simple paragraph on him for I cannot speak of him to this day without being brought to tears. My oldest brother was born with the ability to talk but yet when you are near him you will hear very few words, but his actions speak volumes. He may not always be there when you want him to be, but it's only because he is somewhere else when others need him to be. He has a heart of gold and he is very committed to those he cares for and even those he barely knows. It would take me writing another book to tell you the story of my big brother, one which I may write someday but not today. So I will just say this. He is a man who has been married to the same great woman, my sister Linda, for over twenty years and has worked on the same job for over twenty years as well, which speaks of his devotion and loyalty. During his younger days he was not always so responsible and, like any other teenage kid, he wasted his talents because to this day I still think my brother could have been in the NBA. And he did things that were not right which is between him and the great Judge alone. During his destructive hour he had the consciousness to keep me away from it, and all his destructive ways well out of my sight, leaving me free to make my own mistakes. This makes him one of my great defenders for, had I seen those things, who knows where I would be this day. I think I learned much of my compassion from my oldest brother for he has always been a defender of the underdog. I remember once in high school when these two bullies, known in high school as being tough and somewhat bad, wanted to jump my close friend named Ivan in the school cafeteria. My brother, Lazar stood up and told them it was not going to happen. When they looked at my brother and told him it had nothing to do with him, my brother, all alone in his stance, stared them back down and told them if they wanted to mess with Ivan it had everything to do with him and it was not going to happen. I don't know what happened that day but I saw two of the toughest guys in my school back down for the first and only time. That day I learned a very valuable lesson, which was that sometimes the protection of others must supersede self protection. I have kept that day near me my entire life and have defended others as my brother so bravely did my friend, and you will never hear him speak a word of his deeds.

I remember when I joined the army as a private I did not have much money which did not allow me to come home much, and it was my big brother who found out why I did not come home that much. Once he had learned the reason, every time I would make it home he would say, 'Let's go grab something to eat.' And without a word he would pull up at the ATM where he would withdraw a few hundred dollars and tell me to hold it, and then proceed to *McDonalds* to get us something to eat. Then on to his job where he would have me drop him off only to allow me to use his car while I was home. The first time I tried to give him his money he'd simply say, 'No, you keep that,' before walking off into the brick plant where he worked. Several times my brother pulled up before the ATM only to withdraw hundreds of dollars, giving it to me. I felt bad and I did not want to take his money, but at the same time I was missing my family so much and wanted to come home which was the cause of me being broke. But still I wanted to give it back which is when he spoke these words to me, words with such a powerful impact I could never make it through this story without falling victim to my emotions. That day he told me, 'Hey, it's just money and don't ever let money stop you from coming home. If you want to come home you come home,' and he never said another word about it. When I came home it was always the same. He would take me to eat, pull up to the ATM, make a withdrawal, drive to his work get out and tell me what time to pick him up. There are no words this day or any other day I could ever use to describe the impact those actions have had on my life. Even now to this day I cannot get through this story. My oldest brother, through all his faults as a youth, turned out to be the greatest man I know, definitely one of my greatest defenders.

My next defender was my brother Norman, who was a strange one. He and I were the closest in age, being one year apart, which made us like the cat and dog of the family, because if it was not yelling it was fighting and it was something we did often. My brother Stan was blessed with many talents. He had to be about 6'5" but he was very skinny, I mean so skinny you could see every rib when he took his shirt off, but this skinny guy would surprise you. He could take a football and throw it about 60 or 70 yards easy and the same for a Frisbee which he could throw an unbelievable distance. But far from that talent my brother had a temper that was easily activated. It could be set off merely by just looking at him too long, or coughing on him or by him, even stepping on his shoes would set him off. But along with the temper he also had the gift of music. Music was inside of him and he had been blessed with the abilities to rap and disc jockey. One day my brother and his newly-formed rap group were all in the living room making their own music, and I must say I was really impressed. I remember thinking, WOW these guys are really good. And when I walked in, my brother saw me and a surge of excitement came across him and he told them, 'This is my little brother and he can rap too.'

Now I knew I could not rap, in fact I downright sucked at it. I knew it, but for some reason he refused to see it. So he called me over to the table where all of the equipment was and told them with great excitement once again, 'Hey, my brother can rap, check him out.'

So he gave me the microphone and pressed record on the tape. Now me, knowing I sucked and was about to stink even more because of all the pressure, began to rap as my brother so excitedly had requested. But to my surprise I did not just suck, I stunk up the place on a whole new level. I could hear myself repeating the same sorry one-liner and as I was now wanting to stop my brother just kept encouraging me on, while the look on his friends' faces became hardened with anger. The longer I went on the more angry they became until one shouted out, 'That's enough he's not good he's messing up our tape.'

Now I have seen my brother angry many times believe me because I was on the other end of it most of the time, but never have I seen the look that crossed his face in that moment. When my brother heard those words he jumped to his feet and slammed both fists on the table, sending the equipment flying off the little wobbly table, and began to shout, 'Don't you ever tell him that, don't you ever say stuff like that to him again or I will kill you! Get out of my house, get out and don't ever come back or I will hurt you!'

And without a word, in fear it may be their last, they took off not walking but running. In that moment I thought, Oh God what did I do? Because they were really good as a group, and I began to tell my brother, 'What are you doing? They were right, I am not good. Hey call them back.'

And he looked at me and said, 'Forget them, they are not right, and don't you ever let anybody tell you what you can't do. You are good, and all you have to do is keep practising because someday you will be better than all of us, you'll see.'

So we picked up his equipment and continued to rap and, just as before, I continued to suck. My brother, on the other hand, continued to be excited saying, 'You are good, keep going.'

This, being another one of my stories, has had a profound impact on my life. Because of my brother this is when I began to remove all the doubts and limitations from my life. A few months later Uncle Sam had come and collected me to report to MEPS and then Boot Camp. The entire time in Boot Camp and later in Advance Individual Training, simply known as AIT, I could think only about my family and what my brother had done a few months earlier and I vowed to prove him right.

After graduation I went to my first duty station of Germany and I began to buy my own music equipment, and before long not only had I learned to rap, but I learned to DJ and produce my own music. Having received contracts from three different studios in Germany and won many contest, I now know my brother had seen something in my future that no one else had seen, including me. I had many groups I used to help in their music making adventures, and brought to light what my brother had seen long before me, which was that I was good, I was very good. And from that point no one would ever again place limitations upon me.

Although being a rap star was never my dream I still journeyed to the edge of the dream only to realize that my limitations were non-existent and that I had no limitations. Now my eldest son Boris Jones, who is named after me but in the rap world will be known as Leo Verander, is making his way and transitioning from high school into the music world. And thanks to my brother's belief in me I have obtained a lot of knowledge to assist him when needed.

As parents of four, my wife and I try to follow the examples of our own parents and give passionate opening statements for each of our children. I can assure you they will be very positive and passionate individuals filled with lots of love and encouragement, giving all credit to the Creators for their success and taking full responsibility for their failures while standing behind them every step of the way. The defender opening statements will have a direct impact on the defendant's first dream. The encouragement of the imagination, along with the motivation from the nourishment of the opening statements, will lead to a series of reactions in stimulation of the spiritual inner being to become active, searching the child for his or her special gifts that come directly from the Creators, by the one known as the Holy Spirit. The Spirit will move the child to have a mix of the physical and spiritual being causing reactions in the child's brain in the form of the dream. The dream that tells the child, this is what you will be someday. The child will begin to see all signs point to that in their everyday life, whether it is on the television, in a book, or is a personal experience, which will lead to the most important sentence they will utter as a youth, 'I want to be a ___ when I grow up.'

Now, thanks to my last defender who God had sent to me as an example to follow, my dreams have been fulfilled, for it was my cousin Larry who filled the position of the man I wanted to be like growing up. My cousin had joined the army when I was very little and since it was my dream as well, I looked up to him and wanted to be like him. Every time I saw him come home with the nice car, the muscles and all the self-confidence I just knew that is want I wanted to be. Every chance I got I used to hang out with my big cousin which was great. He filled a missing piece of my life by being there for me every chance he got. It seemed he was never too busy for his little cousin when he came to town. It brings me great sadness to think that my cousin is suffering these days as he has lost his mother and my aunt, Aunt Pug, and not long after that he lost his eldest son and my little cousin. May they both rest in peace.

I would consider myself to be a great success story living the great American false dream, with the big house and cars and other material things, but I would tell you with a great certainty I would give it all up for anyone. For my greatest success in life is and will always be the love of my family. I hold this truth as my most cherished and greatest treasure, and give all thanks to the Creators for blessing me with the greatest defenders ever to be assembled. May the blessings, faith, peace and most of all love of the Father for ever be upon you all.

Chapter Six:
The First Nightmare "The Prosecutors' Opening Statement"

Now it is time for the prosecutors to give their opening statement. They are the ones trying to ensure you serve your time. They are very wise in trickery, and they have had a long time to develop their skills and techniques. After all, they have been around even before Adam and Eve. In fact you know them as the "Serpent", but in the modern day world they will be the ones you call, haters, back-stabbers and traitors. It will be the abusive parent, the child-molesting relative, friends or strangers, and jobless guardian. As they grow older in life their prosecutors will become their bosses, their co-workers, their subordinates and associates and, yes, even their own friends. Sometimes their best defenders in life could and may be their closest friends but this is not the ones I speak of now. I am speaking of those friends and co-workers that would like nothing more than to see them fail. I am speaking of the individuals who will feel they need to bring them down in order to build themselves up. I am speaking of the ones where jealousy has such a hold on them that they themselves have no control over their negative actions. They will make statements such as: 'You can't do that, you never even went to school to learn it'; 'They're not looking for someone with your attitude'; 'You do not get along with others, you are too antisocial'; 'You don't fit in'. While all along they are trying to steal from under them the very life your child seeks. Although they will know all the things they are hearing is not the case, still it starts a chemical reaction in the brain of your child causing them to have sleepless nights, and in some cases start to question their very selves. This is devastating in a very small child since they are pretty much a victim of their environment for the first few years of their life, and their mind is soaking it all in no matter if it is positive or negative. This will certainly have an effect on the child the rest of his life, creating such emotions as doubt, low self-esteem and very little or no confidence in themselves. When your child starts to have nightmares in the night there are bigger forces at work and this is a warning it's time to react. Shower your child with thoughts of love and positive words, and paint a picture of greatness to get them back on track.

I myself have had many prosecutors but the one I will warn you of is the molesting prosecutor. You must beware of who you leave your children with at all times. As small children we were left in the care of our grand momma and although it was not by blood still we came to see her as our grand momma and her kids as our uncles and aunts. In our past, while staying with her, one of her sons named Daniel used to wait outside in the night for the time to come when his mother would force me and my brother to go outside against our wills. We never wanted to go outside because we always knew what was lurking in the dark waiting for us. Although we pleaded with her not to make us go out she never listened and forced us out anyway. Once we got outside it was like me and my brother were in absolute fear wondering from what direction the monster would come. It was as if he was just watching us as an animal watches its prey because as soon as we would let our guard down and think maybe he would not come that night, from out of nowhere he would come. Me and my brother would run as if we were running for our lives but to no avail for he was bigger, faster and stronger and knew he would always catch one of us. I remember when he caught me and placed his knife to my neck with one hand while choking me with the other and told me if I ever said a word he was going to kill me and my brother. As a small child that is a very powerful statement to hear from someone, never mind hearing it under such violence. And while under knife point he made me perform sexual acts on him. I spent my entire life in fear of what I would do to him if ever I saw him again. I lived in fear of leaving my children alone with anyone other than myself or my wife, which may have caused some negative thoughts from within my family, not knowing my reasons. This event has affected my entire life and maybe that of my brother as well as he spent his life going into a rage if someone touched him or looked at him too long. It may be the reason why we have not laid eyes on this uncle for over 20 years. To this day I am always paranoid and have a hard time trusting people. I want to say the words, 'I forgive my uncle for what he did to me and my brother,' but for now the Universe will just have to accept me saying, 'I promise if I ever see him again I won't kill him with my bare hands'. At least I hope and pray that I will not.

So parents, please be on the look out for the prosecutors for they come in all different forms. And although the opposite of the defenders they can have great and lasting effects on your children's lives.

"It's not important who does the planting, or who does the watering. What's important is that God makes the seed grow" (1 Corinthians 3:7)

Chapter Seven:
The Trial Begins "The Corporation vs. Destiny"

'Order in the Court'. When talking about order we are thinking, more or less, of the calm and organization of some things, or individuals and groups. Then you throw in the Corporation and order starts to grow a mind of its own. What started out as a logical arrangement among separate elements of different races and species that once was comprehensible amongst them, quickly changed and became a condition in which freedom from disorder or disruption no longer exists. That which was maintained through respect for the Creators and each other became, in effect, disrupted and completely reversed. Instead of being free of disorder and disruption they are intentionally thrown into creating confusion, public disturbance and complete disarray, along with the lack of respect for one another. Now you are left with only hatred, resentment, hostility, animosity, loathing and horror, which are the tools the Corporation choose to use. In short, chaos has now manifested on Earth.

The Creators created the Universe and all things in it out of "Chaos" and from a disordered state of unformed matter and infinite space evolved the great magnificent Universe that ran in reverse from that which it was born. From "Chaos" we were born into the perfection of "Order" as our intended natural existence, but then came this body of individuals created for the purpose of governing not only the world but the Universe as well which was combined into one body out of many nations and ideas. They are derivative of countless religions and beliefs, from all walks of life, neither from here nor there but of everywhere. They have dissected all aspects of our histories and religions, past and present, calculated the cause and effects, analysed all the risks which are accepted and not accepted. In other words, they feel they can see or control the future from the past. They have learned and recognized the skill in which the Creators have created their greatest works of life through "Chaos", and now have brought this form of creation from the depths of space to the inner sanctum of the realm of the mortal. The Creators have always used such a tool only to create beauty, as it was used in the beginning creating "Light" which began the explosions of all explosions and ended with the beautiful existence of a Universe that works in perfect harmony.

You can see it more closely today. As earthquakes, volcano eruptions and forest fires caused by lightning strikes happen there is chaos in the terrestrial planet inner realm which we also share by feeling its pain in our inner selves as well, of which those shared spiritual woes manifest in us as fear, disarray and confusion. But once the chaos fades you are left with the beauty. From the earthquakes are born the beautiful mountains, from the volcanoes more of the precious ground we walk upon, and from the fires a beautiful mind-capturing forest after it has been modified by the Great Landscaper himself. He so graciously demonstrates his art and craft as he re-grows the vegetation, accomplishing his goal of re-creating a beautiful environment within the torched area.

Even his most precious creation, man himself, is born out of chaos, for from the chaos of birth is born man in their very image.

"Then the LORD God said, "Behold, the man has become like one of Us, knowing good and evil." (Genesis 3:22)

The Corporation realized that if the Creators can create their great masterpieces out of chaos, then that must be the secret and missing equation from their well-calculated formula in which, at some point, all of the greatest minds in existence have placed their works. They realized that the "Theory of Relativity" is real and that all beings that were brought into existence by the Creators are all dependent on the other. Furthermore, they realized their "New World Order" is not just a change but a re-creation. After putting together all the pieces they realized the very beings located on the third terrestrial planet from the "Great Light" that governs the day, are directly connected to each other and all other beings on the other terrestrial planets. That they are neither separated by "Time" nor "Space" but actually all joined together as one by "Space-Time", that which is absolute, that which exists in the beginning, the now, and will exist in the end. That which is everywhere in everything, and of all that is living. It is that which is not bounded by the laws of the physical realm. They realized that the "Theory of Relativity" exists and they realized the true knowledge of it must remain a secret and be kept from man by hiding it out in the open and readjusted to misdirect us all.

They realize if they are going to re-create our very existence they must be perfect in quality, perfect in nature and, most important, perfect in completeness, evading all limits to restrictions and exceptions. There must be no conditions, and the plan must be final, since they would have to leave the body of Christ being disconnected from the whole. This decision must be finite because once they leave the body of Christ it would be written for all eternity resulting in their names being erased from the "Book of Life" only to be replaced with one common identity and to be known by this identity from the beginning of existence to the end of days. The elite group created their "Grand Charter" recognizing it as a spate legal entity having its own rights, privileges and liabilities from those of the Creators' and all that they created. Now, instead of being a part of the "Body of Christ", they are now the "Body Corporate" created to govern or rule mankind. The "Word" refers to them as the "Antichrist".

"They went out from us, but they did not really belong to us. For if they had belonged to us, they would have remained with us; but their going showed that none of them belonged to us." (1 John 2:19)

Now that the plan has been laid, it is time to put it into effect. Those having working knowledge of space-time realize that although on Earth this will take many years, even generations, they also know that in the spiritual realm it is going to take what equates to merely days.

The foundations having been laid, now they needed to begin their recruitment. As a newly-formed group of beings they realized they needed to form a nation, and very specific agencies would need to be formed which are: a Defence Ministry, Financial and Banking Ministry, Manipulations Ministry, Media and Communications Ministry, Educational Ministry, Intelligence Ministry, Technology Ministry, Religious Ministry, Marketing Ministry, and a well established hierocracy.

The Financial and Banking Ministry

They figure in order to pull this off they must first establish a Financial and Banking Ministry whose sole job is to figure out how to get the money. When I say the money I am talking all of it. They must gain a dominant hold on the world's currency in order to be able to manipulate everything from the world markets down to the individual's Social Security and retirement cheques. Once they are in control of the money they will be in a position to influence a large part of the world population, even to cause countries' economies to crash and fall into depressions, which they will.

The Religious Ministry

They will need a Religious Ministry which will be compiled of individuals from all religions under the same roof. They will bring a complete working knowledge of religion as a whole. For how can you manipulate the whole if you have only part of the tool you need to accomplish the goal?

"Beloved, believe not every spirit, but try the spirits whether they are of God: because many false prophets are gone out into the world." (1 John 4:1)

Since this New World Order is also after that which presides in the spiritual realm they realize there is no way of getting around having a hierocracy so the Religious Ministry is certainly a very vital agency. They monitor the religious pulse of the entire world, tracking who is the most dominant, how many members are in each faith, what their principal beliefs are, and ensuring that each faith remains divided because, as the old saying goes, "United We Stand and Divided We Fall". They also are the keepers of the religious secrets which in actuality are no secrets since they reside in all the believers of Christ which we inherited at birth.

In knowing this, it leads me to ask you, what is religion? Really, what is religion and how did it come to be? How many different religions are there? Is religion just another name for faith or is it another name for spiritual beliefs? Is this what we call our spiritual education system or what we call our own re-creation for the Creators' plans for us?

We continue to wear our blinkers when it comes to religion, experiencing the divide while at the same time ignoring it and accepting it as the norm. But how can something so wrong get turned and twisted and be perceived to be so right? Wearing our blinkers is exactly what the Corporation want us to do, giving us the false impression of travelling down the narrow path when, in fact, they're steering us straight to that path that is very wide. And once on that path you will wish that you never wore those blinkers for the wide path is the path that leads straight to the depths of hell.

As I watch the television and see all the different religions I often wonder how there can be so many and how can they all claim to be different while believing the same thing. I often wonder, if in the end you claim to believe the same thing in principle, then why is there a need to call those things something different? Why must there be the need to have a totally different religion? I also understand the simple truth that along with different languages comes different names for things that are the same. I also realize that there are different practices or ways of doing things as a direct result of being from a different culture or way of life. I also understand that the Father created this beautiful mosaic which consists of great complexities and differences which will result in difference practices and rituals creating a whole from many parts. Just as I understand that love and respect should be shown to all parts of the Body of Christ. So, in understanding all of that, why is having a one-track mind an issue when it comes to religion?.

The issue lies in the teachings, for as I watch and I listen and I wait to hear the focus of the teachings shift to the last days, and the great manipulations, sadly it never comes. I watch and I wait for the focus to stay focused on those who are in need but it never comes. I watch and I listen to hear the focus be on the love and compassion of our brothers and sisters of the world but… it never comes. Sure, there are some out there who are doing and teaching exactly what they are supposed to be, and for those few this is not for you. However, we have been warned that there are many sent to deceive us, or who will come and try to teach us wrong. These will be the members of the Corporation's Religious Ministry teams.

We were instructed to challenge those whose teachings appear to be false in nature or not of the truth. But those of you who are wearing your blinkers will be misled as you will miss the wolves putting on the sheep's clothing. You will be leading the pack with your eyes covered, equating to the blind leading the blind and guiding the herd down the wrong path in order to claim your fee per head of sheep, and I am telling you your day will come. Your day will come and when it does you will get more than you bargained for per head of sheep that you led to be slaughter. For those of you who follow out of ignorance, believe me, will not be held blameless for we all were born of the truth and from the truth, for the truth is within us and it is up to us to heed the warnings. We were all forewarned of the Antichrists being in the world as there are many amongst us and they are well versed in their ways and teachings. We were foretold how to recognize those whose teachings are not of the truth but we continue to wear our blinkers accepting all that we feel in our souls to be wrong. You were told to test those who come to teach in these last days. You are required to find out if they belong to the Body of Christ or that of the Body of Corporate. In the end the excuse of not seeing that to our left or right will not save us as we stand before the truth, which is the Father himself.

We are surely in the last days and it is time we turned our thoughts to testing and trying these teachings of the many different religions or beliefs that have appeared before us. There is one true sign and or test which you can always use. Simply raise the question, do they believe in the Son of the Father, do they believe he is the Saviour of man and that he died on the cross for our sins? Do they believe he is the Word manifested in the flesh to

And believe me it's a war that has already been fought and won but must play out in the physical realm for it has been written so shall it be. They will have warriors willing to die for their cause and their numbers will grow at great speed, for their ranks will be filled with those of the non-believer. They will remain steadfast and undeterred in their cause for they will truly believe they will inherit the Kingdom of Heaven. Their sole mission will be to learn the "Art of War", how to adapt to any that they shall face for they are in training for the battle of all battles, the one that shall be fought in both the physical and spiritual realms. They will specialize in a rude form of physiological operations or terrorism where they will kill indiscriminately, for their charge will be to plant the fear in the hearts and souls of man in an attempt to get them to join their ranks. Life will mean nothing to them for they will not understand that they will be only pawns in the grand scheme of it all.

"But you belong to God, my dear children. You have already won a victory over those people, because the Spirit who lives in you is greater than the spirit who lives in the world." (1 John 4:4)

They will never understand the big picture nor will they ever be accepted into the true ranks of the Corporation for their goals are to rule all that exists in this realm and the next.

The Manipulations Ministry

They worked very hard to create their Manipulations Ministry whose charges are to develop a working relationship with the outsiders or those who have not yet fed into their faith or beliefs. They will also deal with the world's reporters, discharging any questions of their legitimacy, and other media representatives, attempting to maintain a deceptive appearance of a world community relations programme, engaging in talks with other countries and their governments, and keeping internal and external communities informed on intentions and threats that may affect them. They are expected to coordinate with the appropriate heads of ministry prior to releasing information to the media on conditions that might result in favourable or unfavourable world reaction, including releases and public statements involving demands, intentions, threats and ownership of their successful attacks. Manipulations leaders are responsible for preparing information relative to their warriors' participation in terrorism attacks, staged world events and political uprising matters, through News releases, Internet websites, photographs, radio and television, and other informational material. They will also review materials such as speeches, News articles, videos and radio and television shows for harmful reviews and integration with the objectives of the Corporation, and determine appropriate discussions. They will create the dialogue and act as rhetoric creators for their public face speakers. They would even go as far as creating the individual's public face and how the world will see them, for their image must be believable. They will create ideological lectures; produce the ministry propaganda newspapers, magazines, and videos to be distributed.

"But if someone claims to be a prophet and does not acknowledge the truth about Jesus, that person is not from God. Such a person has the spirit of the Antichrist, which you heard is coming into the world and indeed is already here." (1 John 4:3)

The Media and Communications Ministry

Their Media and Communications Ministry will be charged with creating and or developing their own media and telecommunications networks to broadcast and push their ideological way of thinking out to the world. It is very important that they are able to push their doctrines and beliefs of their hierocracy and religious mindset from one end of the world to the next. Their ideas must be received in some form or another by the world masses in order to convert as many of the Creators' sheep as possible. So when receiving such rhetoric, you must be wary of wolves in sheep clothing.

"But you have an anointing from the Holy One, and all of you know the truth." (1 John 2:20)

The Indoctrination Ministry

Their Indoctrination Ministry will consist of many. They will be positioned throughout the world and there will be no real substance to what they are teaching, but the message will be that of religion in nature. It will not be an education system of the type you have grown used to, nor will it be an organization in the sense that you may be used to. It will be that kind where the "Word" was manifested into the flesh and walked in the realm of the mortal is mirrored to the extent of sending out their own apostles to travel to the four corners of the living and all in between spreading their ideology. They will have mastered the process of inculcating ideas and attitudes, while they teach by repeating the same message of hate over and over again, being very transitive in their ways.

Since they would have dissected every part of our past, present and perceived future, learning all they can about history and human nature, they will also indoctrinate some through cognitive strategies or, with precision, it will take on the traits of a professional methodology. As in everything there is always a way to tell the difference. If, in fact, someone is trying to indoctrinate you or educate you then simply by questioning the doctrine or critically examining it will reveal to you what is happening. For if you are being indoctrinated these acts cannot and will not be allowed. They will also use pejoratively, often in the context of political opinions, theology or religious dogma. In others words spew out a doctrine relating to matters such as morality and faith, put out in such a way it takes on an authoritative nature by a church using all sorts of hatred in their words, with the belief that they are the absolute truth.

I say let them have their negative connotations for their day will come when the masses will realize that something is missing or unseen as if there was no light to guide them through the darkness and this simple realization will begin to light their path. And where there is light, darkness will scatter, for the light will overpower the darkness. They will speak but nothing of substance will be heard for their hearts will be evil in nature and their souls of the darkness. So where our Lord Jesus Christ and his apostles spoke from the light, the Corporation apostles will speak from the dark. As Christ's teachings spoke of love, compassion, mercy and service to each other, theirs will be of the opposite. As the dark is to the light so will their words be to that of our Saviour. They will preach hate, violence, no mercy, and self-service to gain the gratitude of the Corporation who will have promised them eternal life. And, most importantly, they will not recognize the Saviour as the Word and Son of God that was manifested in the flesh to live without sin and to die for ours.

"Who is the liar? It is the man who denies that Jesus is the Christ. Such a man is the antichrist--he denies the Father and the Son." (1 John 2:22)

As Jesus spoke of the Father and his blessings, they will speak of another whose name is not yet mentioned but will be known to all as the "Antichrist", and the false blessing he will bestow upon them.

"You were bought at a price; do not become slaves of men." (1 Corinthians 7:23)

The Intelligence Ministry

They will have a form of Intelligence Ministry whose sole purpose will be to acquire and supply to the other ministries secret information about another race, religion and nationality, or their potential enemies. Instead of an agency, or office staff employed to gather such information, it will be a network of normal individuals embedded all over the globe, mixed in with all the different walks of life. They will have the ability to learn without being educated, and will be very successful in adapting to new situations so no matter how hard we work to change our tactics they will be able to adapt as well. They will be skilled in reasoning and problem solving due to the fact that their entire lonely existence will be behind enemy lines, whereby they will show they possess superb verbal abilities, extraordinary social competencies while being very effective at adapting to any one of our environments and new situations and changes that may take place within them. They will infiltrate our homes, our offices, our clubs, our churches, our social circles, and even our very families. But if we are weak and lose faith they will infiltrate the most important part of us all, our very minds which will inevitably lead to our very souls.

"Then he remembered his dreams about them and said to them, "You are spies! You have come to see where our land is unprotected." (Genesis 42:9)

The Technology Ministry

Their Technology Ministry will appear to be behind the times when in fact they will have some of the greatest technology at their disposal. They will have facial recognition cameras, radio frequency identification chips, sophisticated voice recognition equipment, cameras that broadcast on both analogue and digital frequencies, digital cameras mounted in every computer, every phone, every television and every car, home and GPS system. They will have super-computers that will be faster and more intelligent than any ever created, which will monitor the world conversations, e-mails, and everyone's location. There will be a mergence of the world's currencies forming one standard currency in which they will also place micro radio frequency dots, and later create a digital currency which will be placed on radio frequency data chips that will hold all of one's life information, along with their allowances for their works. The chip will be created to be implanted inside the body of the living.

They will continue to create new technologies at an astonishing rate with the sole purpose of tracking and controlling all life on Earth. They will create a very specific logo for all the property they create so none will be confused. The logo on all their technology will be the name of that which is to come but the name is not known yet nor the number of his name. To all he is known as the "Antichrist".

"He also forced everyone, small and great, rich and poor, free and slave, to receive a mark on his right hand or on his forehead." (Revelation 13:16)

When the Corporation and all their ministries are fully in place the real battle for truth will begin. You will try to fight this injustice unarmed but I must warn you, you will not be able to win. Sure, you will fight with much bravery and courage but the only weapon that will be able to help you is that which we all were born with. This weapon is the most powerful weapon in existence capable of ending all wars, all crimes, solving world hunger, providing shelter for the world's homeless and ending all hatred if applied correctly to the foundation of life itself. It is the most sacred of commandments that was not of the original ten that were written in stone but could have been found in the underlying meaning of all ten combined and later deemed so important that it was hand-carried to us all by the Son of the Father, Jesus himself. This is the secret that the Corporation fears; it is the secret they don't want you to know. It is the most secret of secrets, the holy of holies, it is the power of Unconditional Love for each other. This is the weapon that can save us all. When going through your journey in the Great Prison of Life love will be your greatest weapon. Love your brother and sister; love those who hate you as well. While you are facing all your trials of life remember two things, which are: all is possible through the Son, and to love one another so much you would be willing to make the ultimate sacrifice for your fellow man and woman.

"Dear children, let us not love with words or tongue but with actions and in truth." (1 John 3:18)

Our lives are on a predetermined course and the events that have been set in motion are beyond our power or control. Since it has already been written and promised by the Creators, it is the inevitable or necessary fate which all things both physical and spiritual are destined to witness. Our true destiny has always been that of faith, unity, harmony and love, but just as there has always been dark and light, actions and re-actions, there will exist forces that will oppose our true destinies.

"Praise be to the God and Father of our Lord Jesus Christ, the Father of compassion and the God of all comfort, who comforts us in all our troubles, so that we can comfort those in any trouble with the comfort we ourselves have received from God." (2 Corinthians 1:3-4)

Chapter Eight:
The Trials for the Segregation of Love

"We love because he first loved us." (1 John 4:19)

I once asked the question how many different types of love were there and what an interesting question it turned out to be. It was a question where the answers will surprise most, to include myself, as I received numbers ranging from one to twelve.The names of the different types of love I feel are not important. What is important is how we have let the enemy come in and dissect that which we have received from, in the beginning, the Creators themselves. The Corporation took the purist emotion of all and broke it down and categorized each piece until now instead of one there are many. Then they threw on a name to each piece and dressed them up as a whole, and now some feel its okay to feel one and not the other. But I am telling you IT'S NOT OKAY.

"This is the message you heard from the beginning: We should love one another." (1 John 3:11)

This is a very important trial that we all need to be aware of since the verdict will affect us all. This is a dangerous precedent to allow to be set, for all that is and all that will be will be determined by this very emotion. The events have already been written, and will surely come to pass, but the underlying question is what side of these events you will be on? The enemies have a very interesting technique when they want to hide very important things or confuse the masses. They simply place that which they desire to hide directly out in the open. They simply break down the information, rename the pieces and then throw them at us and, sadly, we will begin to fight amongst ourselves claiming our piece is the original, or the best. We will continue to fight each other while the enemies sit back and say this is too easy. They underestimate us while the Creators continue to believe in us, and while we continue to let it happen. Well, I will make this very simple for you. One LOVE.

"God is love." (1 John 4:8)

There is only one LOVE anything else is just that, something else. Some say the Bible speaks of two different loves while some say three, but I am here to tell you some things were changed in the Bible by man, this is why the Creators gave each of us all the knowledge in our Spirit.

I listen to people as they explain the different types of love to me as they see it, with a straight face, and all I can do is just listen in disbelief. I am not trying to be critical and judgmental of others and if that is the case then I must say okay it is what it is for there is no other way to put it nor will I try. Love is very simple and I will explain it this way. The Father tells us to love as he love us, and we are to keep his love, and love will be very important in the end days, which we are now in. We are supposed to love each other to the extent where we would give our life for each other.So I ask you, how can you love one more than you love the other? You have something greater than your life itself to show a greater love for someone else. Where is it written that it is okay to place conditions on your love?

"And he has given us this command: Whoever loves God must also love his brother." (1 John 4:21)

God loves the world so much that he sent his only Son to walk among us and to die for us. The Creator himself is Love, so are you telling me there is more than the one Creator and he lied to us when he said he is the one true God, the Alpha and the Omega?

"Whoever does not love does not know God, because God is love." (1 John 4:8)

I will leave you with this, there is no such thing as lustful love, conditional love, security love, or even friendship love. There is only HATE or LOVE, you choose. You can call it what you want but in the end it is what it is. If you have your lustful love, when the end comes all will be stripped away and all you would have left is LUST. If you have your conditional love, in the end when it is all said and done all you will have left is your conditions which will fade away with the things of this world. If you have your security love, then in the end you will have nothing for all the materials of the world that were provided to make you feel secure would have faded away leaving you with nothing. If you have friendship love, then I tell you this is foolish because love is love and if you loved your friends and not your enemies then in the end it will be known you did not love, for anyone can love a friend, but he who loves his enemy knows God's love. What we call unconditional love is not the name of the Creators' love this was the Creators' way of explaining their Love. Love is love and they want us all to love unconditionally, which is to love without conditions, without titles, without classifications, without choice of who to love, but to love all and everyone just as they love us.

"This is how we know what love is: Jesus Christ laid down his life for us. And we ought to lay down our lives for our brothers." (1 John 3:16)

There is no one person more important to love than the other person. Each person has their place and treatment which may be different according to their place, but when it comes to love, that is the one true constant that unites us all. For love is the very spirit which we all received from the beginning and the spirit is the Creator. So have your enemies, have your friends and be the friendliest one can be; have your husband or wife and join together and become one, loving them as God loves the church; have your parents and honour them and add length to your life, but when it comes to love, love them all the same, which is more than your life itself.

"And I am convinced that nothing can ever separate us from God's love. Neither death nor life, neither angels nor demons, neither our fears for today nor our worries about tomorrow--not even the powers of hell can separate us from God's love." (Romans 8:38)

Chapter Nine:

The Trials for the Separation of Love and Compassion

Love is now under attack by the Corporation and in the end they have lost the battle but yet they will continue to fight, for they truly believe that through our weakness they can win. They have carefully thought out their plans and seen the future and seen that they will rule. Even if it is for a short time they still will rule. They are chipping away at the very foundation which holds us all together. It is so amazing they know what combines us and we do not know ourselves. We have lost our way and our faith and in the end some of us will have lost that which unites us to the Creators themselves. We must be very careful as to what knowledge we receive and learn, for the true knowledge we have already inherited at birth but the additional knowledge only confuses some which in the end will cause them to lose their inheritance which is the promise of eternal life.

"Dear friends, let us love one another, for love comes from God. Everyone who loves has been born of God and knows God." (1 John 4:7)

Another tactic the Corporation will use is the domino effect, whereby they knock down one little domino and that one knocks down another and then another until all have fallen bringing down the whole group. During this trial the first domino name is "Compassion", whose sole purpose is to link all of mankind in their suffering which creates a strong desire to stop the suffering of others and, in turn, their own suffering. For one to feel compassion they must be filled with the Spirit for how can you possess such love without he that is love itself? There is no greater virtue one can possess then the virtue of compassion, for when this emotion is felt one does not think of oneself but solely the suffering of another which is the greatest attribute of love. Without the ability to feel the suffering of your brothers and sisters how can you follow the commandment of the Creators to love your brothers and sisters and ease their suffering? The Corporation knows this so they begin to chisel away trying to remove the compassion from mankind, for they know if they succeed it would rip away at the very fabric of love itself. Today you see evidence of this everywhere from the immigrations issues, to people getting evicted from their homes, individuals stepping over the homeless on the streets without a simple hello, never mind sharing a little money for them to buy food.

"How great is the love the Father has lavished on us, that we should be called children of God! And that is what we are! The reason the world does not know us is that it did not know him." (1 John 3:1)

I've seen reports on television where the hospitals had been putting sick individuals out after their insurance limit was reached, putting them in cabs while still in the hospital gowns only to be dropped off in alleys. Now where is the compassion? That is beyond a lack of compassion, that is in line with pure hate.

The greatest evidence I've seen of the corroding of compassion was during the crashing of the twin towers in New York City. In certain countries people danced on the streets as thousands of human beings died a tragic death at the hands of individuals who claim they love but love not. Sure, everyone in the world has been wronged in some shape or form and many have died a useless and unnecessary death in the belief of making the world a better place. But there will never be peace on Earth as long as we continue to lose sight of that which is important. When asked what is important some will say numerous materialistic items but I say unto you that those things are nothing. Sure, we need them to live but far more than any of that what we need is to keep that which was given to us since the creation of man. What I am speaking of is that which is in all of us and bonds us together as one, that which makes it okay for us to have our differences, but still be able to live in peace. What we need to remember as we cheer as others are dying in some distant land is that with each life that is lost due to the heartless and ruthless killings, a piece is chipped away between love and compassion. When the world finds itself turning without love and compassion, then the other dominos will also fall as we will lose our sympathy, empathy, pity and love, and as they fall they will surely transform. They will transform from the light to the darkness, turning to cruelty, harshness, indifference and then hatred.

"Anyone who hates his brother is a murderer, and you know that no murderer has eternal life in him."(1 John 3:15)

Search within yourself for there is the truth and the truth is love and to have love there will be compassion. And hold on to it, share in the pain of your fellow beings and ask yourself, what can I do to help? What you think, "little or nothing", could not be further from the truth when dealing with love and compassion for it is not in the amount since there is no amount, but in the act itself.

Take two men, one being rich and the other homeless and poor. And in this example the rich man is stripped of his love and compassion and when facing the homeless man they both are sure to die. The poor and homeless man will die of loneliness and starvation here on Earth for without companionship and food how can he live? The rich man, although he will be quite comfortable here on Earth, when the end comes so will his comforts and materials of the Earth end and his lack of compassion to the homeless, starving man shall be remembered. Instead of eternal life with the Father he will not be accepted for he did not know Love and Compassion here on Earth, nor will Love and Compassion know him in the hereafter.

Now take the same rich and poor man, only this time the rich man sees the dying, starving and homeless man that he does not know but feels his suffering and decides he must act or surely the poor man will die. The rich man tells the poor man that he has a warm place for him to stay and all the food he can eat, and the poor man accepts the gifts and thanks the rich man but also thanks God. The rich man smiles, with such great warmth and emotion that falls upon him that he could not describe. And just as promised, he feeds and shelters the poor man, and they become great friends. Now, not only shall they both live but they both have gained an unbreakable bond of friendship. They both will live comfortably here on Earth for they remembered Love and Compassion and kept it close and when the ends comes, Love and Compassion will remember them both and just as they found comfort on Earth so shall they both find comfort in the hereafter. Love and Compassion towards one another is the solution for what appears to be all the unsolvable issues here in the physical realm. Without it there is one truth that will remain, wide will be the gate of the condemned while narrow will be that of the saved.

"If anyone has material possessions and sees his brother in need but has no pity on him, how can the love of God be in him?" (1 John 3:17)

Tampering With the Jury Pool "Here are Your Blinkers"

During our creation our Father has paid much attention to details, as he so generously gave us our six senses, and the tools to utilize each one of them to perfection. Sure, sometimes some of our tools fail to work but by the grace of the Father he supplied the work-around. For if we lose one of our senses he so graciously multiplies or increases the capabilities of the others to make up for the one that was lost. We have been given the greatest gifts to use as we go forth and do the Creators' work. We have been blessed with a mouth to fully taste the delights that were given to us for nourishment and to communicate with one another. A nose to smell the heart-tempting fragrance of the nourishments, and all the great fragrances of the world, as well as that of our carefully selected mate. We have been blessed with ears so as to hear the sweet sounds of the Earth and each other. And we have the sense of feel. To be able to feel the soft touches of our mate and or pets is certainly a blessing that is so wonderful to have.

Then there are the other two that we tend to take for granted as we look to them only as to the obvious but not to the full extent as to why they were given to us in the first place. The senses I speak of are the gift of sight for both the physical and the spiritual realm. We have been blessed with two eyes so we can see all the beauties of the Creators. This is not just the seeing of all the beauties of the land, oceans, air and space, but all the beautiful and wonderful things taking place within them. The sixth sense grants you the vision to see within the spirit realm, which is important for it is the spirit that connects us all and to lose this vision is to be lost and left feeling all alone.

Each and every one of us may find certain sights, sounds, smells, tastes and textures more pleasing than others. There will be some smells that we find rather bad, while someone else may find that very smell pleasing, and the same goes with all the other senses. What you find to be painful another may find pleasurable, and what you call noise I may think of as sweet music. When it comes to sight we must be very careful for sight of all things is always that which the Creators intended us to have, which is why we were blessed with the ability to see in both the physical and spiritual realm.

Because the sixth sense is not that of the physical realm then the tool itself is not visible upon your body or head. Although you cannot see it with the eyes of the physical realm it does not mean it is not there. And it does not mean the signals being received from this tool will translate to be seen, heard, smelt, tasted or felt from the other tools. What it means is its transmissions could only be received in that which houses our very spirit, our inner being, our very soul. It will only register in our thoughts and intellect, our very consciousness itself.

Well, as part of the Corporation's grand scheme of manipulation they have found a way to slip blinkers into your babies' gift baskets. And, as we all grow up, we see this gift as something special as it allows us to just focus on what is happening in our own lanes, ignoring that of our brothers and sisters and the very Earth itself. They realize that to get us to a state where we would be susceptible to change they must separate us from that which binds us all, which is the spirit of the Creators which is found in us all. These spirits have several names, taking on several different forms. We know it as the Holy Spirit, the very spirit of the Universe, the light that was created by the spoken word of the Father, the Word, our spirits, our soul, and most of all Love. Blinkers, also known as blinders and winkers, are that which was created for horses to maintain their focus to their front by taking their sight from the sides. I use this term because most of us have accepted our blinkers from the Corporation and have begun to wear them with pride. And as we journey through our trials of life our visions have now become obscured. We are happy as we go about our life, focusing only on what is to our front or in our lanes and ignoring everything else. This is harmful because, through the wearing of these blinkers, our senses of sight in both the physical and spiritual realm becomes narrowed and blurred which has a substantial effect on our ability to show love and compassion for our fellow beings, including the planet itself. In the breaking of this connection we are in fact corroding the very fabric which binds us not only to one another but to the Father as well.

When I started wearing my blinkers is unknown but still at some point I found myself wearing them and now even until this day all the things that I thought were not visible to me are all I see as they haunt my deepest thoughts. I remember when I went to Germany my first time as a new private in the army we went on a tour down town in one of the cities, and there was a man sitting on the side of the streets who appeared to be homeless, begging for money. When I went to give the individual money the person who was in charge of the tour said to me, 'He probably will eat better than you tonight'. At the time I wondered what she meant as that was the only comment made as she walked away. The comment stayed with me for years but still my heart had always compelled me to continue to give just because of how the individual was dressed and looking. In a sense it made me feel pity for them. Well, for many years I continued to give to anyone I saw or walked by on the streets who looked less fortunate than me and appeared to be truly in need. I would just simply, without speaking, reach into my pocket, giving them much of what I had or even sometimes all of it depending on how they looked and how I felt when I saw them. For some made me feel more of a sense of urgency and compassion then others.

Then as I grew older and was back in the States stationed in Colorado I was driving down the road when I stopped for a traffic light and saw this gentlemen who appeared as if he was very much in need of some assistance as he wore a cardboard sign around his next which said, “will work for food”. So I rolled down my window as I always have done and gave to the man, and my friend who was in the car with me said, ‘You know, that man is making a good living off people like you’. What he said echoed heavily with me for it reminded me of what the tour guide said in Germany almost a half a world away and that is when I adopted my own saying. I told him that it’s okay because if I gave to five individuals, four may be a fraud but at the same time maybe the one out of the five is truly in need. And isn’t it worth giving to the four frauds if the one who was truly in need received as well? I always feared that if I hardened my heart because of the frauds that some day I might miss the ones who were truly in need.

Well, again several years passed and I found myself home in Columbia South Carolina for vacation and me and my mother were walking into the store when I saw a man standing outside the store who really looked like he was down on his luck and he was asking for some money. So again I gave the man all I had in my pocket and that’s when my mother said some of those individuals are not what they appear. She said maybe I should have offered that one food or something else. Now my mother is probably one of the most caring persons who you could ever meet, after all, she is the very source of my compassion next to the Creator himself. So when I heard it from her you could imagine what I was thinking at the time. I found myself wondering what could make my mother think this way? So I told her why I feel I should not pass those who are in need, and she told me she would never ask me to do such a thing. She said, 'Giving is good, it's just that to some of those individuals it's a job and the way they are dressed is their uniform. All I am saying is you can always buy them food or give them clothes and if they are in need they will be just as happy and thankful.'

Well, we proceeded into the store and I decided to go back out to the car and what I saw I believe is what made me begin to wear my blinkers. When I went outside I saw the individual whom I'd just given all the cash from my pocket on the sidewalk with another individual dressed in the same manner as him. They were both smiling and laughing, counting a great big wad of money. When I saw that, in that moment all that was said to me in the other countries and the States began to ring clear to me. I realized that everywhere I had travelled in numerous countries and the States I had seen over hundreds of these individuals on the streets and sidewalks and I remember thinking, my God how can they do such a thing, are they

Well, for a few years I struggled with giving to individuals on the street, sometimes I gave and sometimes I did not. I had in fact begun to wear my blinkers. I asked the Father every time I passed someone on the streets who appeared they were in need, was I wrong, should I have given? I mean it really bothered me inside if I passed someone who appeared to be in need, in fear I was passing by Jesus himself. Each time I raised the question in my mind or to the Spirit I received the same response. I was always reminded of the story I heard when I was little. Who first told me the story I fail to recall, however, it was one I would never forget. It was the story of the woman who had asked Jesus if he could visit her, and as she walked she encountered three individuals in three different situations. One needing water, the others food and shelter. They looked destitute but yet she turned them all away in their moment of need for she was wearing her blinkers and was focused on one thing and one thing only which was the visit from Jesus. After a while she realized Jesus was not coming, at least that is what she thought, so she asked him why did he say he would come but did not. And he replied to her, I did, I came three times and each time I came to you, you turned me away. It was that story when I first heard it in my youth which made me the type of person not wanting to pass anyone who was in need and it was that same story the Creator always used to answer my question when I wondered if I was wrong for passing someone who appeared to be in need.

There are many stories that I can credit with giving me the excuse to put on my blinkers such as finding out some of the charities that were raising money for the starving children around the world only made their founders rich, as they would give the minimum to that for which the charity was created while lining their pockets with the rest. Then there is one story and only one which I would credit as allowing me to see that the wearing of blinkers is wrong, which is the story of Jesus and the woman who wanted him to come visit.

I say to you all, if you see someone in need as you walk on the streets think not if he is a con artist, but instead think of the priest, the Levite and the Good Samaritan. Think only, what if he is truly in need and because of the evilness in the worlds that manifest as the con artist, frauds and crooks that the person you are about to pass will starve that night? Also think that maybe in that moment you have been praying for Jesus to come into your life and when he did you missed him because you were wearing your blinkers and passed right by him on the streets when he came to you.

I asked the Father can I keep them, I told him they were great because they allowed me to see only what was to my front and allowed me not to be distracted or frightened by that which was to my sides such as the priest and the Levite had done. The answer I received was the same as always which is the story I fore told and I received understanding of the Father's reply to me as being, it's okay to enjoy your blinkers just as long as we know when he comes he will come from all sides and angles not just the easy and straight path. And those of us who choose to wear our blinkers so proudly will never see him coming.

Witness Tampering "See No Pain and Suffering"

Every day of our lives we bear witness to some type of pain and suffering of others, in some cases we will even be the direct cause of it, yet we pretend not to see it. Is this the world as a whole? No, it is not but the number of individuals who look the other way is growing with each passing day. It's almost like the human race is starting to grow tired of caring. How could such a thing be when it is supposed to be hard-coded in us all to care for one another more than we would care for ourselves? How can we live in peace while ten minutes down the road our brothers and sisters are being terrorized? Easy, for if it doesn't affect our little circle then in most cases it does not pertain to us. Our blinkers are on and they are working great.

I often think of the scenes on national television of New Orleans after Katrina hit and it breaks my heart. To see all those people on the bridges and the roofs of their homes, and the dead lying in the streets and floating down the streets just tore me up inside. I watched on in horror knowing that this is truly a sign of what's to come in America, and around the rest of the world. During this moment in time I realized that there are a lot of officials in our government who are now wearing their blinkers with great pride. I realized that the power has officially shifted from the people to the government and we don't even know it has happened. I realized as I listened to people talk that while some made me feel very proud of the human race as they wanted to do all they could to help, including opening their homes to some of the victims, there were still some who actually had the nerve to criticize the people for living there and not moving. As if a whole city of people can just pick up and move.

I also remember seeing the images of the people dancing in the streets of the foreign lands while thousands of people were being crushed to death as the twin towers were brought down on top of them. I listened as people tried to argue that their pain and suffering were greater than the others'. I also listened as people justified ignoring someone else's pain and suffering all because in their past or history they themselves or their race had suffered as well.

At this rate there will come a day when the whole world will experience great pain and suffering as we continue to let this negative energy grow out of control. We will come to learn this valuable lesson once it is too late that although the wearing of our blinkers may appear to be good as it allows us to focus on that which is in front of us and not see the fears and or threats to our left and right, in actuality we are allowing that which is to our left and right to grow and dig in until one day it will be too late. We will be consumed by that which grew to our sides while we focused just on that which could only be seen to our front. Sure, I know there are a lot of crooks, frauds and con-artists out there but there are also a lot of good people out there as well. When someone is in pain or is suffering it's time we rose as a whole. And I am not just talking about one or two nations I am talking about the world. Every individual on the planet that is able to come together in some form or another showing the power of love and forgetting that which divides us and return to that which unites us.

Sure, everyone cannot give to every charity every time, but in the end there is more than items and money that can be given. There is always your time. Seek out a place in the privacy of your own home and pray for those who are suffering, for when the whole comes together in prayer, what was once thought has the ability to become mass and matter. For those of you who have destroyed your blinkers this is not speaking of you for you are not wearing your blinkers. This is for the ones who never gave to anyone in need and doesn't plan on giving. This is for the ones who once gave but for some reason or another have turned to the darkness and refuse to give any more, stating they have given enough.

Hear my words for as sure as I am writing these words for you, things are going to get worse. Life on this planet will become unbearable, and those of us who had not suffered before will experience great pains and suffering. And those who had suffered before will be the ones we will need to turn to for help because they would already have the experience in dealing with it.

Love and compassion are the truest form of energy, for this is what your very soul is composed of and it is the very soul of the Universe which I also like to refer to as One Harmony. Our love for each other along with our compassion are the very elements that are used to bind us all together making one body out of many. Simply put, when you use your blinkers to avoid seeing the pain and sufferings of others you are actually disconnecting yourself from the whole, and to disconnect yourself from the whole is to also lose your connection to the Father. For ignoring those who are suffering is to ignore him and his commandments. Even if you cannot do anything financially or materially, still in seeing it and feeling it you are doing far more than you can ever imagine.

If you think this is solely about you going into your pockets, wallets or purses and giving money then you will be wrong. This is about keeping our connection to the Father and not letting the Corporation strip us of our love and compassion towards each other. This is about you actually looking and feeling the pain and suffering of your brother and sister for we are one and we are all connected. And they will in turn feel your love and compassion as you feel their pain and suffering. When this happens, although you are away from that which is causing the pain, you experience the pain while you are in comfort, while those who are in discomfort will experience the love and find comfort while going through their suffering. In essence, you are switching places with those who are suffering by freeing their mind through the spiritual realm. Remove your blinkers and look to your left, right and rear and see those who suffer, feel their pains, sympathize, meditate and pray that they would find comfort in the arms of the Father. And if we all do this as a whole and at the same time then those who hurt may continue to suffer in the physical realm till help arrives but in the spiritual realm we shall all comfort each other.

The Pain and Suffering of a Terrestrial Being

We often wrap ourselves around the pain and suffering of human beings and even some of us can feel the need to stand up for the pain and suffering of animals, but the defenders of the 3rd oblate spheroid from the sun are few and far between. Sure, there are some out there who are taking a stand and coming to the defence of the terrestrial being we call home but they are only a few. They need us to remove our blinkers when it comes to this great keeper and caretaker of life and in one voice, in one thought, in one prayer ask the Father to help in the healing of this honourable caretaker before it's too late. I know you may be wondering what this terrestrial being has to do with us wearing blinkers... Well, it's quite simple actually, the more we ignore the pain and suffering of this terrestrial being the more we as human beings will suffer.

Let's try a small demonstration or experiment with the use of your body. Now I say the use of your body because I would not dare try this with my own. So let's use yours and with the help of a few tools let's create a small pump about the size of a stick pin. Once we have created one let's duplicate it and make a few hundred thousands. And let's take these newly created pumps and put them all over your body, in your heart, neck, legs, arms and head and then let's turn them on and begin pumping out your blood. For the sake of the demonstration let's just call them blood wells. Next let's modify a few of those pumps and place them on your throat and chest, extending the length to reach down into your lungs and begin to pump the air out of you and for this experiment we will call these natural air pumps. Let's not stop there, let's drill down to your bones and start pulling out big chunks of the bones and, oh, the liver looks important, let's grab some of that as well. As we begin sucking and pumping everything out of your body faster than you can recreate or heal what do you think the end results will be?

Sure, you can argue that the planet is not a living being but then I would say to you that the mosquitoes and gnats can also argue that the huge chunk of moving flesh they are sucking on, receiving their nourishment, is not living either. The bacteria and viruses that enter our body and grow spreading throughout could lay claim that we are, in fact, their planet and yet it does not stop us from saying we are living, and paying the doctor to rid us of the bacteria, viruses and diseases. Well the planet is no different.

Although we human beings are a part of the terrestrial being's inner self it still does not stop us from having a cancerous effect on her with all of our machinery, vehicles and buildings. More especially all of our oil wells, natural gas wells and so on. I use the example of cancer not to make light of this terrible disease, which is taking more life on this oblate spheroid than any other disease with the exception of heart disease, but because the effect we are having on the Earth is one and the same. Cancer is actually a part of our inner self that somehow has gotten out of control and is beginning to do it's own thing. It is considered a disease of the genes which happens to be a part of our most basic foundation and building blocks that make up the human existence, or any other living creature as well, for it is a small part of our DNA. Like all workers in any shop have a title, so does it, for it is the Master Molecule of the cell. The job of the genes, also known as the Master Molecule, is to make proteins which are the worker bees of the cells for it is their proteins that allow our bodies to operate according to the intended designs allowing us to walk, run, think, pray or even breathe.

Throughout our lives the cells in our bodies are growing, dividing and replacing themselves, as many of the genes produce their proteins which are involved in controlling this process.Something can occur that will trigger a mutation in the DNA molecule which can disrupt the genes and produce faulty proteins. This causes the cell to become abnormal and lose its control on growth. What happens next is what I would call the man-made effect, for the abnormal cell begins to divide uncontrollably and eventually form a new growth known as a tumour or neoplasm. Do you see the resemblance to the cause and effect we as humans are having on this honourable being? If not then your blinkers are working great.

The human beings are like the cells that are growing, dividing and replacing themselves, while the Earth's atmosphere, weather and inner defences such spawns act as the genes producing their version of proteins in the form of the natural selection of diseases, illness and environment which serve as a control over our growing, dividing and replacement, also know as births. Just as with our DNA, a mutation occurs in the Earth's DNA, the part of the DNA that is us humans. The mutation is the wearing of blinkers and, just as inside us, it disrupts the genes and produces faulty proteins which cause cells to become abnormal and lose control of growth causing them to divide uncontrollably and eventually form a new growth known as cancer. As I mentioned before, the wearing of blinkers is our mutation that causes selfishness, self-indulgence, arrogance, greed and idiocy. These in turn create the cancerous effects of having many babies out of wedlock and so multiplying the human race abnormally, building extremely grand structures that house nothing but the owners' egos, spreading to the deepest parts of the seas or most extreme outreaches of the Antarctic in search of fossil fuel. And we create more and more artificial creatures of the sea and fowl of the air that take in more of the terrestrial being's oxygen and in return replace it with carbon monoxide and other deadly gases instead of carbon dioxide, the natural gas that is critical to her survival. While we are replacing this much needed gas with poisonous gasses we continue to spread to the rain forests and jungles and continue to cut down the very thing that naturally creates the gasses the terrestrial being needs to breathe, like a cancer growing in her lungs. There are over a hundred forms of disease that fall into the cancer group and we replicate each and every one of them as related to the Earth. From skin cancer as we continue to destroy the Earth's atmosphere which is its protective outer layer, to cancer of the kidneys, taking away her ability to filter out the waste and poisons in her fluids as we secretly dump toxic chemicals into her water supplies and landfills which eventually soak down into her hidden water sources. Just as in a healthy human being the immune system can recognize the neoplastic cells and destroy them before they get a chance to divide, so do the Earth's defences try to do the same, resulting in tornados, hurricanes, forest fires created by lightning strikes, earthquakes, typhoons, cyclones, some diseases, along with heatwaves and cold waves and more.

However, some mutant cells may escape the immune detection and survive to become tumorous in nature which, as in the human body, are of two types, benign or malignant. The one that is benign is not considered cancerous, for simply ridding itself of it will suffice for it is slow-growing and does not spread or invade surrounding tissue. However, just as the human body has malignant tumours which are cancerous so does the Earth. Malignant can be a nicer name for it but is also known as the stupid, as the unprotected playboys and easy females, as a large part of the wealthy, not all but a large part, the manufacturers, the world's defence agencies, the irresponsible chemical industries that secretly dispose of their waste illegally, and so on. No matter how many of these negatives you rid the world of, they will continue to return. They invade surrounding tissues and spread to other parts of the body and so do they when it comes to the Earth.

Many have come before me trying to explain the theory of relativity which we just don't get or refuse to acknowledge but I will make it real simple for you. If it is not man-made it is then linked by nature with man-made objects, becoming a major factor exerting great influence over the natural making it to relative. If you think of that last sentence as being false in nature then I will show you how the circle comes fully enclosed. As we spread and damage the Earth as a form of cancer, in return most of the cancers in human beings are caused by changes in the cell's DNA because of damage caused by the environment. That's right, this is what we call karma, poetic justice, ironic or simply the truth. The terrestrial being or environment creates many types of carcinogens which are responsible for causing the initial mutations in our DNA. That's right, imagine that... the Earth is using cancer to fight cancer. So while we continue to suck the planet dry of all of its natural resources before it has had the chance to heal, while the rest of us so proudly wear our blinkers and look the other way as we fill the Earth's lungs full of smoke and deadly gases, remember one thing - what goes around will surely come around.

Do I expect the world to go back into the Stone Age and get rid of all the technological advancement? No I certainly do not, for the blessing of advancement is from the Father himself as it is natural to continue to improve upon that which is. Nevertheless, what I expect is for us to come out of the Stone Age and again do as we were meant to do and create better technology, cleaner fuel, less unneeded concrete jungles and more natural jungles in an attempt to make the world better for our brothers and sisters and our children and their children. Do you know that compared to the knowledge and know-how of yesterday we are currently in the Stone Age and refuse to leave since the Stone Age resources are so profitable to the wealthy and harvesters of the gains? It's time we removed the blinkers and started demanding that we come out of the Stone Age and move into the New Age and start tapping into the New Age resources of water and hydrogen. There are some who have rigged their cars to run on water, while there are many who think creating fuel out of hydrogen is cleaner, cheaper and more bountiful, but most of all better for the planet. While there are some who are already harnessing the power of the sun, there are some who believe there is technology out there that is far more capable of producing substantial power levels from water, wind and sun while the greedy and wealthy muffle their efforts. We all know the days of fossil fuels are long past their expiration but we would rather see the planet blow up before demanding better alternative fuels.

While we continue to ignore the pain and suffering of this great and honourable terrestrial being, keeper of life, she will continue to take evasive measures to cure herself of its malignant objects. Just as we blow our nose when it runs, sweat when we overheat from viruses and bacteria that cause us to have temperatures, bleed when we are cut, tremble when we are cold, have muscle cramps when they are over-used or lacking water or oxygenation, so does the planet when it is reacting to things that irritate, overheat, suffocate and overload her. Just as we speed up and shorten the length of our lives by overexerting ourselves, so do we as we overexert, overuse, and undernourish the planet. Just as we all have an expiration date, so do all the terrestrial beings of space, and there will come a day when our mother in spirit, for the flesh of man was created from her, the beautiful terrestrial being, the 3rd oblate spheroid from the sun, who is the keeper of human, animal, sea and vegetation life alike will begin showing signs that old age is catching up to her. She will begin to grow tired and slower in her old age, as her rotation will cease to be what it used to be, and her ability to keep the harmful rays out and filtration of the dangerous gasses in her air will weaken. Her ability to hold herself together will also grow weaker, which will in turn cause some serious natural disasters far greater in strength than any we have seen.

Everything that men have created was modelled after something in nature. There is nothing that men have, can or will create that the Father himself does not hold the original patent to. Everything conceptually, from cars to the atomic bomb, was a derivative of nature. So, knowing that piece of information, what happens to a car engine when it overheats or when the load is greater than it was designed to handle? Or you try to operate it after draining all of the fluids out of it? All things that are living require some form of substance to survive, and the Earth is no different. It's not too late to begin to repair the damage but first we need to remove the blinkers and see the damages. For in nature everything requires the acknowledgement of the problem, before the path of recovery can be travelled. Does an alcoholic not first need to admit being an alcoholic before any treatment can begin, just as a sinner must admit to the sins before asking forgiveness? Well, we all must first admit we are destroying the planet and voiding the warranty prematurely. We must realize that not only are we one with each other but we are one with this great and wonderful terrestrial being the Father named Earth, along with all the other celestial beings linking the inner beings with the outer, making us all one known as the Universe, or what I like to call "One Harmony".

Chapter Ten:

The First Recess "The Crossroads"

You will enter a recess period providing you with some time to readjust your strategy or get a breather. But what you will not know is that this is more than just a break. It's a pause at your first crossroads of life. Which road you take readjusts your entire path, journey and, yes, even your destiny. You must choose carefully, but fear not, you are not alone at this time. At this time you will feel the Spirit with you more than ever for although you can reset your destiny, your true destiny has already been written, and it is the Creators' will that you live out your true nature and not the misguided one reset due to lack of knowledge or misdirection from the Corporation.

I have come across many crossroads during my trials and journey, and each time I felt a strong desire from within nudging me in a specific direction. My first crossroad I remember from when I was very young. Me and a group of my friends were sitting around talking, and it wasn't long before one pulled out what I believed to be a cigarette and lighter. He lit the cigarette and began passing it around the small circle. After a few individuals, who we will call exhibits A, B and C, took their hits it was passed to me, and in a split second my life flashed before me at lightning speed. After seeing the light I decided not take a hit nor pass it any further and simply threw it to the ground and stepped on it. I often wonder what type of effects that simple moment in time would have had on my life. Sure I have crossed many crossroads and I have found one thing to hold true in most cases, just staying straight is often the wise route. If by chance you truly feel you have to go in a different direction then keep this in mind, always follow the path that is well lit, staying in the light at all times. If you can remember this and stay away from the dark paths then you will encounter no problems too big to handle during your trials in what is your journey to eternal life.

It is all of our true destinies to reach the end of our journeys and stand before the one and only true Judge and be found righteous and receive a pardon from the death sentences that the Corporation slew of judges have passed down in their unauthorized preceding.

"Even though I walk through the valley of the shadow of death, I will fear no evil, for you are with me; your rod and your staff, they comfort me." (Psalm 23:4)

"For who among men knows the thoughts of a man except the man's spirit within him? In the same way no one knows the thoughts of God except the Spirit of God. And we have received God's Spirit (not the world's spirit), so we can know the wonderful things God has freely given us." (1 Corinthians 2:11-12)

Chapter Eleven:
The Great Manipulation

We now live in a society where we are all constantly being tempted and manipulated. They have entrenched us in this false sense of security, coupled with undeserved trust, and like a herd of obedient sheep we follow without question or, even worse, with the wrong questions. There has always been one who has been chosen to speak to the masses and from his mouth you will feel the truth for the truth will be with him. We do not recognize a simple truth, which is we are all part of this global science experiment where the Corporation is trying to see if we could all actually co-exist on a global scale in unity with regards to nationalities, race or gender. They are trying to see if their New World Order would work according to their plans. They know it could be done for it was they who were the cause of the separation in the first place, and now they want it back, only they want it back without the love and spirit of the Father.

Well, after establishing the framework for their plan they have to create their greatest masterpiece which would be the foundation on which their plan would be laid. First they have to create a whiteboard, or fresh canvas, and to do this they need to wipe away all forms of government and start afresh. To do that the entire mission must be devised in great secrecy, and a cover would have to be established in order to answer any questions that may arise. Then you would need to find a location to establish this prototype of the new world order. Once the location was found and all forms of government and law, or in other words order, were removed then and only then the foundation and cornerstone could be laid.

Regardless of what one may think in principal, it makes perfect sense creating a world where everyone lives in harmony and peace with regards to race, nationality or faith. After all, this was the original plan of the Father. However, the Corporation saw it as a threat and destiny has now been written so, of course, what started out as harmony quickly became tarnished and corrupt, for they want this one whole without the love and the Holy Spirit. The Corporation saw that peace and harmony was good and they could use this to their advantage, so what was always joined had quickly become separated and, just like that, religion was not recognized on a national scale. Also, to ensure there was no more genius in the midst, the great numbing of the mind began, for they know to control the masses they had to control their hearts and minds. They began painting on their whiteboards or canvas, quickly outlining what was to become their masterpiece.

The original true and just founders describe a government of the people, for the people by the people, always considering the people. And for a time it appeared to be good, but in many ways it was flawed. Still the project went on according to plans and had appeared to be a great success. The people were happy and prosperity flourished for most but definitely not all. Although the little experiment seemed to be a great success the heart of man was not righteous for there was no true unity in a land that claimed to be united. As we broke the covenant with the Creators to love all our brothers and sisters we began to bring shame to that which in principle was very honourable, whereby the implication of it was indeed not. There was an entire race regarded as savages, slaughtered and uplifted out of their homes and land, destroying their very societies and way of life but never their spirits. How can they have claimed to be just and righteous before God as they brought on the pain and suffering of a people who had appeared to be living at one with the land? Then they followed that up by kidnapping an entire race of people placing them in the holds of the ships where they died of illness and diseases. And the ones who survived lost their classification as human beings and lived a life of great pain and suffering, being whipped and beaten. They lost their rights to learn and grow mentally, while some were hung and killed at the whim of those claiming to be righteous. Those were not the only group of God's children that were left on the outside only to be killed and buried in the very foundation of the New World Order. The foundation of the New World Order may have been laid on top of the just and righteous but it definitely was not laid by them unless they were forced to do it through slavery.

Question… How do you control and maintain order of a group of individuals that are thrown together from different races, religions and nationalities? You create a system they hate more which would bind them together as one only to hate the other. For a better form of control, used for manipulation and control, you will need to create one or more systems for them to hate.

During my time in the military I had been in charge of many individuals or groups of individuals but what I noticed was that the more individuals in a group, the more race, nationality, religion and colour made a difference. I had finally worked my way up the ranks receiving the rank and title First Sergeant, receiving my first company consisting of 140 soldiers. I quickly discovered it was not the same as being in charge of the smaller elements such as a section, squad or platoon because all the discriminatory factors increased as the like factor numbers grew. This created an issue since like groups started to group together and the team factor fell victim to the separate group factor. And since we knew we were going to deploy to war I had to develop a plan that would unite all theses separate groups into one whole, creating one team out of many groups.

My plan was really simple actually, which was to create a figure they all hated more than each other. Next, I had to implement a control whereby I could release what I then called the beast or the less-liked factor of the whole. So, since the hated person had to be outside of the whole, while at the same time being head of the team, naturally it would be me who filled that role. Next, I needed a control, something that would not be well received. I found the perfect control which not only would help in the team building process, but also it made them stand out, served as a source of motivation, and created an atmosphere that was high in discipline. The control I chose to use was the singing of military cadence. It was perfect actually, it was something that had to be done by the whole and no matter how loud or how good they sounded I could always say they were not loud enough and punish the whole group together. No one was outside the limits of the punishment, including myself. To be a true team we all had to suffer together. Next I had to implement systems that ensured every single need of the soldiers in the whole was met, or at least a true effort was made at meeting the needs of those that could not be met. Next a truly balanced reward and punishment system had to be put in place. No one part of the whole could feel or perceive that another was being treated better than they were. Then I had to find out what would make each group happy, and what made them angry.

Once all my data was gathered and my plan was carefully thought out it was time to implement it. First, I quickly made promises to solve those issues that each group saw as a demotivating factor and followed it up with action solving each of the issues. Next, for the things they thought would raise the morale I quickly implemented courses of actions that put those things into effect. Now the foundation was set they learned this guy can and will make things happen. Next they learned if I said I will do something it will get done. So now that I had them believing in me it was time to tilt the scale in order to bring balance, because too much of a good guy act can be just as harmful as not enough when leading the whole. In order to bring balance I had to release the beast and allow the whole to meet their nemesis. So I introduced them to their new requirements that I knew would not go over well. They were directed to be standing in formation formally 10 minutes prior to my time for company formations and 20 minutes prior to time during the battalion formations. While out there, one had to come up front and sing cadence while they all marked time in place, singing at the top of their voices as we all had to do in basic training. And believe me, most of them hated it then and in a company where that was not supposed to happen they certainly hated it once again. Of course, you got your usual mumbles and low singing and improper marching in place but it was good because, little did they know, it was exactly what I knew and wanted them to do.

The first day I gave them warnings all day as I smiled on the inside but held a stern face on the outside. The next day was the same at which time I gave them another warning and told them about the beast that is held in a cage and the only way to keep him there was with the loud and thunderous sound of sweet cadence. The third day could not have been any more perfect to introduce them to the beast. It had been raining the entire day before so the nice green grassy field with the dark brown dirt underneath was ripe for the occasion. Once we came from our 4-mile run I marched them over to this field, which had to be about 150 metres in length, and began to have them low crawl, high crawl and perform three to five second rushes. Before long we were all completely covered in mud and we did this for an additional hour after already completing an hour of physical fitness training, after which I ordered them all to be back to work in an hour. So basically this took place on their time and they had to change and eat before returning to work.

This process was repeated for another two days because, as I said, they were not going to be loud enough unless I said they were loud enough. I continued to pile additional requirements on to what already seemed to be overboard but the additional requirements were also designed for their benefit, even though at the time they did not see it as that. I required that each of them learn the Soldier Creed word for word, and then the 10th Mountain Song, then the Army Song, followed by the NCO Creed, which was a question that most missed on the promotion boards. This meant that by learning those things at that time they did not have to learn them prior to the boards. I had them to say these things in unison along with the singing of the cadence. Even though they were not seeing the transition, all the other units and commanders along with our leaders noticed a big difference. A company that was plagued with issues prior to this new system all of a sudden had become this extremely motivated, well disciplined team. And what once had many issues now barely had any. The internal fights were now replaced with laughter. The once discriminatory factors now became unseen as they finally bonded into one team, one of which I was honoured to have had the pleasure of being their First Sergeant.

This ability to form a company that had issues into a highly motivated and disciplined team earned me the distinct honour of serving as a First Sergeant over three different units in a two and a half years span, serving over all three in a combat zone fighting the war on terrorism.

Now let's flash back to the original question of how you get the different groups of people to co-exist. Easy, you create a villain which, instead of each other, they will hate. Then you put the controls in place that can raise the discomfort level of the whole. So what or who are the villains of the group in this New World Order? As I mentioned before, it had to be someone outside of the whole but part of the team in a position to implement change, in other words the government. This reigns true of every nation on the planet, where they have to form such a ruling power that unites and controls the team. However, this is more so about the prototype of the New World Order. The original government or plan was meant to be one government of the people for the people and by the people, but the Corporation saw this as the perfect opportunity to lay their foundation to take over the world. Instead of a government of the people, for the people and by the people, we ended up with a multi-branch, multi-party system that cast the illusion of being separate parties when in actuality it is indeed a government system that only projects the illusion of being separated. This was established for the sole purpose of controlling the masses while creating more of a one team one ruler concept. In short, while the people are too busy choosing sides of a more structured group, they fail to realize that the sides they are choosing are of the same whole. So while your individuals of the old world of the white picket fences, oven mitts, great jobs, great economy, so-called moral values, and racist tendencies choose one party, all the misfortunate, mistreated, and all others choose the other party. Now, there are those few that are either confused, or know something is just not quite right with the party system, who choose another. Then you have those that just don't know or haven't a clue and just jump in wherever. Now what you have is a group of people who think that they are with a party that is against the other when in fact you have created a system where the villains and the heroes live together in somewhat perfect harmony. However, there are times where harmony must be disturbed in order to maintain balance, so what you get is a little chaos intentionally thrown into the harmony to disrupt the order or else the whole will start to wake up and see through the male cattle faeces. Now you have your New World Order living together in harmony in regards to the discriminatory factors, and in all actuality in a reverse non-order kind of way, which means their New World Order is in fact an old world without order, just a better plan.

Every day we leave our homes and go to work with our blinkers on, never stopping to question the very system that was supposed to take care of us but has failed so many. How can you have one of the richest nations where more than ninety percent of its wealth belongs to less than a half percent of its population? I say it's time for the people to wake up and take back the government which was created for them. This is the time, while we have someone leading the nation with a pure heart that is loaded with compassion and love for all of the children of the Earth. My only fear is that this will be a missed opportunity because of certain media organizations and groups of people and their inability to see beyond the colour of his skin.

"As for you, the anointing you received from him remains in you, and you do not need anyone to teach you. But as his anointing teaches you about all things and as that anointing is real, not counterfeit--just as it has taught you, remain in him." (1 John 2:7)

Chapter Twelve:
It's "Elementary"

Many of us attended some form of school in the physical realm, some never attended, and some reach only as far as elementary, middle or high school before dropping out for whatever reason. Some of us went on to complete high school and receive our diplomas or general equivalency diploma, while some chose to reach for higher learning and attended some college or completed a degree of some sort online. Then you have those that have the gift of extreme intellect with 3 or 4 degrees. Whatever your education level is I think it is safe to say we have all achieved it here in the physical realm, in an educational system that was designed to numb our minds and implant their ideological beliefs in everyone. There has never been anything that happened in any of today's societies that was not carefully planned out and implemented for the benefits of the Corporation, including the women leaving the home in search of so-called equality and their careers. I am willing to bet it was the Corporation who was truly behind the women's movement, manipulating the whole thing in order to get them out of their homes where they slowed the process of manipulation by being at home filling their kids heads with the knowledge of true love and compassion and seeing a well balanced home consisting of a loving mother and father. Getting rid of the mother from the house would ensure that the education systems had more influence over the minds of our children. I often wonder how they got away with not teaching religion in the schools, since 75 to 80% of our entire childhood is spent in school. Well, as I said, I may wonder but I am not surprised since in the end it is all about religion. Well, it's time we went through a little re-education, only this education will not be conducted in the physical realm but in each of your spiritual realms.

There are those who have actually received their PhD in the spiritual world while there are some of us who chose to drop out a long time ago. But however long ago it may be it is not too late to return, so let's do that. Let's take a short trip back to school which will take place in the land that was, is and will be and there will be no teachers or instructors from this world. Your education level means nothing in this school and there will be no one grading your answers, and all homework will come from yourself so you may be able to take your time or cheat if you must. But know this, all work will be graded and in the end you will want to have this diploma. There will be no human teachers, no materials needed unless you see fit to write something down. Nothing is needed because these classes will be conducted in the spiritual realm and all work will be that which you deem necessary to assign yourself and even though you complete it in the physical realm it will still be graded in the spiritual world.

The education system you will be going through consist of one level and this one level only, which will simply be known as "Elementary". You may be thinking why elementary and no middle or high school, and why not all three? The answer is quite simple. To the Universe the knowledge you are about to learn is basic knowledge, because there is no higher or lower but only the knowledge itself. Second, the knowledge may be the same but relates to every individual differently. Elementary simply means being able to relate to something on a very basic level because it is very easy to learn and, since its fundamental or in its simplest part, it is easy and not complicated. You need to look at each question as if there is something hiding behind the question itself.

Since this school will be held in the spiritual realm there must be a form of trigger to send you there. And what I believe to be the best trigger is questions, for answering questions induces one to think and to think is to journey in one's mind which is the gateway from the physical realm to that of the spiritual. The deeper the thought the better the learning experience will be.

Now please don't simply read and answer the questions, for if you do, you have done nothing more than read and answer questions of the physical realm and you would have learned nothing and would have received only the manipulative answers of the Corporation in return. Meditate on the question, sleep on the question if you must. However, just know that each question should be taken very seriously and you should expect an answer to come back to you in your dreams or random thoughts. Believe very deeply you will get an answer. Don't pray for an answer because God has already given you the answers. Just look deep inside yourself and find the answers you seek, and as sure as I sit here typing you will get your answers. I can generalize why you would not get an answer but I won't because if you truly seek an answer then an answer you will get.

"But you have received the Holy Spirit, and he lives within you, so you don't need anyone to teach you what is true. For the Spirit teaches you everything you need to know, and what he teaches is true--it is not a lie. So just as he has taught you, remain in fellowship with Christ." (1 John 2:27)

QUESTIONS

Question: Is there truly a God, or Creator?

Question: Where did we (Man and Woman) come from, and what happens to our consciousness and intelligence after death?

Question: Where did our form of intellect come from?

Question: What is the Soul and do other creatures posses one?

Question: How can our inner being just disappear into nothing or non-existence after our death?

Question: What is Love? Is there more than one type of Love? Is Love real?

Question: Is there other life form in the Universe or are we all alone?

Question: Do I love and care for my family? How do I know and what did I do lately for them to know it?

Question: Do I love and care for all human life? How do I know and what have I done lately for others outside of my circle of family and friends?

Question: When was the last time I showed some form of compassion?

Question: Do I truly love my wife or husband? What must he or she do before I file for a divorce?

Question: Do I love with or without conditions?

Questions: Am I a racist, or atheist, and if so how did being such improve my life and the life of others?

Question: What is the true religion?

Question: When was the last time I showed someone true kindness? Go out and do a kind and selfless act for a total stranger. How did it feel?

Question: Do I need credit when I perform a kind act, or am I okay with going unnoticed for the deed?

Question: When was the last time I told my children I love them and that I am proud of them? Do they know without a doubt of your love?

Question: When is the last time I told my parents I love them. Do they feel your love?

Question: Do I make myself available to my parents when they need help and, if so, do I perform the help with great joy in my heart, or bitterness?

Question: Are your kids proud of you? Are they proud you are their mother or father?

Question: Should I give to those you are in need? How much is enough when giving to those in need?

Question: Do I give to my friends when they are in need and, if so, how do I feel afterwards?

Question: Do I have any enemies and, if so, why? Is it because of me or them?

Question: What have I done for my enemies lately? Would I give to them just as generously as I would give to a friend or family member?

Question: How do I feel about people from other countries?

Question: Do I think I have made a difference in my lifetime, will my name be remembered?

Question: If God came tomorrow would I be ashamed to look him in the face?

Question: Did my ignorance make the world, the country, the neighbourhood, my kids, or friends better in any way?

Question: Did I chase my dreams or did I just settle for anything that came my way?

Question: If my life was to come to an end tomorrow, would there be anyone at my funeral?

Question: Is my life everything I thought and wanted it to be?

Question: What is my limit? What can I not do? What do I want to do? What is stopping me from doing it?

Question: Do you believe in Jesus and if so who is he?

Question: Can you ask God for forgiveness in Jesus' name, and believe you will receive it?

Question: If the doctor told me I had one week to live how would I feel, what would I think, and most of all would I be scared?

Action: Today, if you are able to find someone who is in need or is suffering, show them some kindness and when asked why, simply reply, 'Why not?' and walk away.

Action: Today, if you are less fortunate than others, tell a complete stranger you love them and wish them many blessings. When asked why, simply reply, 'Why not?' and walk away.

To get the answers to the above questions and more, all you have to do is believe, concentrate, focus or meditate, and you will find the answers and more. Life is life and it will be until death, but until death visits we all should live life to the fullest. A lifetime can feel like an eternity when things seem to go wrong, but then when times are good it seems to speed past us. So you must know life is too precious and too short to waste. Find your peace, find your comforts, and find your joys, and once you do, share it, share it with your friends, your family, but most all share it with your enemies. Love and compassion are free and bountiful so please don't be stingy, feel free to give and show all you can.

The last lesson is the simplest of all but will be the hardest to perform. This last lesson is that we all must love each other, friends, strangers, family and enemies alike. How do you know when you have received knowledge from the spiritual realm and how do you know the knowledge is real? Well it's very easy, since you have inherited the truth at birth from the Holy Spirit it is already inside you so when you receive clarification in the spiritual realm you will automatically know it's the truth and it is good. It may come to you in many ways but no matter how it comes it will come from one location, that being the spiritual realm. Therefore, you may receive the answers in your dreams, daydreams, a thousand-mile-stare moment, or a sudden thought that just interrupted your normal thought process. But whichever way, it will come when it is time and you are ready to receive it. It may even come by way of a messenger, a book, a movie, or an animal. No matter how it comes you will know it to be your answer. If you are looking for answers just to troubleshoot the process then the answers will forever escape your grasp, for in that moment your heart is not openly and honestly seeking the truth but instead is seeking that which is for the wrong reasons. Don't be afraid to seek your answers and once they are received you are then charged with the sharing of your understandings with others, laying the seeds which will for certain help others to grow. Just be cautious of the foundation on which you plant your seed, for the seed that is planted on or in the wrong foundation is set for certain failure and will not grow, in some cases causing more harm than good. Also, you must be very careful of the seeds you do plant for, as every farmer is held responsible for every crop they harvest, so will you be for each of your crops harvested from the seeds you laid. Always remember we are sent only to plant and water the crops but the Father will give them life and make them grow.

Some people have the gift to receive this knowledge and some have the gift of prophecy and in most cases if you reveal such information to those you already know from birth and childhood they may look at you like you are nuts. Sometimes it is better to take your knowledge and share it with those who have not known you and it will be well received. I find that simple statement to be loaded with the truth because since I have been travelling throughout the world I find when I speak to those who do not know me I will draw a group of focus listeners trying desperately to receive every word. Some may not agree but they listen very closely, sparking a discussion that for certain invites the Holy Spirit in to clear up all misunderstanding, to bring those who are true in heart to the universal understanding which is also simply known as the truth. Where two or more gather in search of the truth, so shall the truth gather to fellowship with them.

Chapter Thirteen:

The Prosecutor Argument Begins

The prosecutors of the world are all those who oppose you throughout your lifetime. They will come in all types and forms, but their true form is of the negative energy of the Universe and they do not know what they do for they themselves will be lost. They are merely being used as a tool for the enemy in this eternal battle between good and evil. The individuals possessing this energy will manifest in many different but familiar forms. They will be: family, friends, strangers, enemies, employers, employees, co-workers, and also the evil spirits that enter you as well. The greatest weapons you have at your disposal are kindness, love and forgiveness.

I have encountered many prosecutors in my lifetime and I found that combating them with emotions of the physical realm will not be enough. Sometimes we must be wise and just know when to depart the situation and just walk away. The prosecutors will come at you in many different ways and you must be smart enough to see it. Never claim the victim role because in these instances there are no victims there is only negative and positive energy which is not bound by the rules of the physical realm, whereas the physical aspects which result from the energy are.

Now you are probably wondering what in the world is this author trying to tell me? And if you are one of the ones thinking this just know your scepticism will be well founded. Let's take your friends and enemies. This is the simplest form of the negative and positive energies which in these forms are very easy to spot and, furthermore, deal with for in most cases they hold no advantage point over your life. A friend is nothing more than the opposite of an enemy but when it comes to the negative and positive energy of the Universe it is not so simple. For instance, a friend can produce just as much of this negative energy as an enemy and, vice-versa, an enemy can produce just as much of the positive energy as the friend. Just because you call someone an enemy or a friend does not mean they are a good or evil person. That physical title is just a boundary of the physical realm and is simply a direct relation to yourself. But in the spiritual realm the one you call friend could be rotten to the core, or in his very soul, whereas the enemy could be that of love and compassion. This is why you need to see the prosecutors for what they truly are, which is the form of negative energy from the Universe. In other words that which is the opposite of good and is not bounded by the rules of the physical realm and in its true form it feels no remorse, guilt, sympathy, nor compassion, because it's true form is evil. Evil knows nothing of physical emotions, for its very being is without such physical attributes that are found only in humans. Evil is the negative energy inside the physical form and although the host may feel these emotions after he or she has committed an act which they deem to be shameful, hurtful, or violent, the negative energy will not as it is the cause of effects only. Just look at the prosecutors as an entity which is incapable of feeling anything. To relate its spiritual form to the physical realm, look at the persecutors as being the sociopath of the spiritual realm with zero emotions, no fear or remorse, just the sole desire of being evil without concern for the effects of its actions on the Universe.

I have had many who claimed to be my friends and at some point I realized the energy that came from them was very negative. They betrayed me and once I noticed that their energy was negative in nature I simply cut my ties with them. And although I felt a great urge to get revenge I knew all I would be producing was more of the negative energy and I would have assisted in the cultivating of their seeds. Instead I chose to let the true keeper of revenge take care of that as I simply swept their seeds off my armour which prevented them from taking root.

I remember being stationed at Fort Carson Colorado and while there I had this individual who I had always related to as my enemy. He would do anything in his power to make me look bad. I am talking about the works; talking behind my back, verbal attacks to my face, making false statements about me. It grew so bad that it got to the point where we almost came to blows over it during a training exercise when we were deployed to the National Training Center (NTC). I was ready to attack him and the only thing that saved him that day was a long-time friend named Anthony Parks, known to me as

P-Funk. He quickly saw my anger and knew I was at the point of no return and hurried over and saved the individual from certain pain and injury. Well, we went on with the training exercise keeping our distance from one another knowing that we had reached a point in our existence of failure to co-exist. I continued to ignore him while he continued to talk negatively about me to his friends.

A few days later the exercise was over and it was time to go home. After being away from home so long you realize how much you miss the simple things of home and come to a whole new appreciation of those things. Well one of the things I came to appreciate was the heater in my car. At this time I had just purchased a brand new car which was a 2002 Chevy Impala LS fully loaded with everything they had to offer, including leather seats. As I was riding back in my cold military truck on this dark, cold, rainy night barely able to see out the window, all I could think about was how I could not wait to get in my brand new Chevy Impala and crank up the heat and make my way home to my family who were waiting for me. As usual, we all had to drive the vehicles to the motor pool and lock them up and from there we would get in our POVs (Privately Owned Vehicles) and go home. Well, as we all left the motor pool on that dark, cold, rainy night the road had a long line of soldiers from our company making their way home. When leaving the motor pool, to get off post everyone travelled in the same direction proceeding to the first light and making a right turn on to the road leading off post. Unless you were impatient. Then you took the right prior to the light, crossing through the parking lot of the *U-Haul* rental agency and up the small hill through the small shopette parking lot and then turning right on the road leading off post by passing the stop light. Well, as I was proceeding to the light, which was taking a while to get to due to all the cars ahead me, I was just thinking how great it was to be in the warmth of my car. And as I got closer to the light I noticed a set of headlights pointing down towards the ground. As I got closer I noticed they were from a small yellow pickup truck, and then I realized it was the pickup truck of the guy who was my enemy. It was the very guy that only a few days earlier I had threatened to snatch the spine out of his neck for verbally insulting me.

Unknown to the members of my unit, while we were away they had dug a trench the entire length of the *U-Haul* parking lot in preparation for laying wire or pipes of some sort. Being impatient, my enemy had decided he would avoid the light by taking this route through the parking lots, and shortly after entering the parking lot he drove his front wheels directly into the trench causing him to get stuck. What I also noticed was that all of his friends he was talking negatively about me to continued to drive past him leaving him stranded in the night not able to get home to his family. His very friends felt no compassion or anything that would cause them to stop and help their friend. Once I came closer to the opening of the parking lot I saw him dressed head to toe in the old military green wet weather gear which only provided protection from the water to a certain degree but none from the cold. I felt very bad for him so I turned into the parking lot to assess his situation, which is when I saw the trench that had been concealed by the dark of night and the rain. I got out of the warmth of my car and asked him if he was okay, which is when I noticed the shock and surprise on his face as he stood in disbelief as to who stopped to check on him. While he continued to stand in shock I kneeled beside his vehicle, without wet weather gear or a jacket for that matter, to check out the damage. There was none and all he needed was some assistance to be pulled from the trench.

Without delay I told him to get in my warm vehicle that was still running with the heater on, and I told him I may have some cargo straps I could use to help him get out of the trench. He looked at me and then my brand new car and refused to enter the vehicle since we were muddy and wet and had nothing to cover the seats. I simply replied to the man, who I was now seeing not as my enemy but a husband and a father who had been away from his family all this time and who had been out in the freezing cold and was now wet and miserable, to get in the car. I told him, 'It's only a car, so tonight let's worry about getting you home to your family and tomorrow I will worry about the car.'

Still hesitant, he got in the car, sitting very straight and still as if it would keep the water and mud from getting into the car. So to relax him a little I began to talk to him saying how I did not even notice that trench so as to ease his mind, letting him know it could have happened to anyone. When he mentioned he had seen his friends but none had stopped, I carefully told him, 'Well, it's dark and maybe they just did not notice you', which we both knew was a lie but one he so gratefully accepted. I began to make jokes which caused him first to smile as he fought to hold back the emotions of laughter, but then as he no longer could fight the positive energy he began to laugh. From that point we spoke as friends and not as enemies.

We returned to the motor pool and I retrieved the cargo straps and then drove him back to his vehicle. He then tried to get the cargo straps which I consciously placed on my side of the car behind my seat. I took the cargo straps and told him to get in his car. He said, 'You don't have wet weather gear and it's my mess let me.'

And I told him, 'No, get in your car.' I climbed under the rear of his vehicle, wrapped the cargo straps around the rear axle and then as I was walking back to my car to do the same I told him to start his vehicle. I slowly pulled him out of the trench and once he was out we got out of the vehicles and unhooked the straps. He began to thank me and apologize about my car, and the hateful things he was doing to me, and I told him to get in his car and go home to his family and to forget all that mess.

That night one of my most hated enemies, in fact at that time my only enemy, became my friend. I also realized that the man I thought was evil, was in fact not evil at all, but instead a good man going through one of the lowest points of his life. He was losing his wife, whom clearly he still loved very much but who wanted to divorce him, and at the same time losing his home which the court ordered them to sell and split the proceeds. He found comfort in speaking to me about his situation as I always had time to listen to him and spoke only when I thought words of encouragement were needed. We departed Fort Carson as very good friends.

So you see the prosecutors may come in different forms but no matter the form it's not the person but the energy that you are immersed in battle with. The same goes when the energy takes the form of an individual from the family, or your workplace. This is the reason why revenge should be left to the true Judge for if I had taken revenge not knowing the true heart of one of my persecutors I would have unknowingly added to the already deep issues and suffering of another human being. Recognize your prosecutors and cut ties, don't let them ruin you but at the same time don't let them turn your positive energy into negative energy by allowing their seeds to take root within you by seeking revenge, or wanting to cause harm to another human being.

"Thou shalt not avenge, nor bear any grudge against the children of thy people, but thou shalt love thy neighbour as thyself: I am the LORD." (Leviticus 19:18)

The Prosecutor Argument Continues: "See No Evil"

Sometimes it is very easy to blame others for all the negative energies of the world when the true culprit can be found by taking a glance in the nearest mirror. Sometimes in life we'll find that we can be our own prosecutor, responsible for the bad things that affect not only our own life but the lives of others as well. As we will continue to discuss, there is always a cause before each effect, or reaction for every action, which is why some of the worst actions or effects will be brought on us by no one other than ourselves. Please allow me to provide a few examples of how our acts of self-serving can come back onto ourselves.

The Death of a Child

Mrs. Johnson felt her mind beginning to wander as she contemplated, what do I say? Oh God, if I tell what really happened maybe Leroy will come after me next. But Lord, he killed that woman's baby and he needs to go to jail. Suddenly snapping back to reality and realizing she had to answer the officer's question, she replied, 'Hey Mr. Officer I did not see a thing.' Mrs. Johnson felt her heart start racing as it began beating with great force and, although she knew it could not be, she began to think the officer could see and hear it as it pounded in her chest as if it was trying to alert the officer to the secret being held hostage within.

'Ma'am,' Officer McDaniel said, 'I'm truly sorry for the assumption.'

'What… I'm sorry did you say something?' she asked.

'Yes ma'am. I was saying ma'am that I just assumed that if anyone would have seen something it would have been you since the street light in front of your home is illuminating the crime scene which can be seen clearly from your window there.'

'No.' Shakes her head. 'Sorry, I didn't see a thing,' Mrs. Johnson once again managed to speak. Clearly she was at odds with something as her mind continued to wander. 'I did not see the man who shot that poor child in cold blood, because I was asleep and when I sleep I am out cold. I am very sorry I could not help you officer.'

He stood in disbelief as he stared directly into her eyes wondering how did she know the suspect was a man as well as knowing the victim was a child if she did not in fact see a thing? He knew he had not said anything about the gender of the shooter. As he allowed his mind to wander for a second he thought, great, just what I need, another frightened witness.

'Okay ma'am. Well if I may I will leave you my card so if anything, anything at all, comes to you, you can give me a call down at the station.'

Good luck with that, she thought to herself, as she reached for the card. 'Yes sir, I will definitely give you a call.'

I won't be holding my breath, thought Officer McDaniel, 'Okay, thank you ma'am and again I am sorry for disturbing your sleep.'

The next morning Mrs. Johnson could not wait till her friend Linda had arrived at the office. 'Girl did you see what happened last night? Leroy came out of nowhere and shot Samantha's baby boy dead in the head.'

'Oh my God,' replied Linda. 'How did you know it was Leroy?'

'I know because I saw him, he was trying to shoot JT and instead shot Samantha's baby. Girrrl it was horrible.'

Linda's heart began to race as her mind began to project images of her son Jason through each of her thoughts. 'Oh my God what did you do?'

What do she mean what did I do, she thought? 'Girrrl I just lay on the floor and waited for the gunshots to stop and then I finished looking at last and ate the rest of my cold grits. And you know how I hate when my grits get cold, that really makes me mad.'

Cold grits, did she just tell me she was worried about cold grits? Lord what is wrong with this woman, thought Linda.'Johnson, what did you… did you tell the police what happened?'

Is this cow for real? 'Child no. They came knocking on my door asking what did I see and I told them I did not see a thing, I was out cold and when I sleep I don't hear nothing.'

What an idiot, Linda thought! 'Girl I know that's right, you know Leroy is crazy."

The Theft of a Neighbour's Wages

Mr. Jacobs opened the door with a sense of urgency as he quickly entered the waiting room of the Emergency Room. He felt all eyes in the room quickly turning and focusing on him but he did not care as he felt a great anxiety sweeping over him as his heartbeat continued to increase in speed. 'Excuse me ma'am, sir, ma'am,' as he walked through each of the rows of chairs as if he was desperately looking for something. As he was looking, his eyes met with the eyes of what appeared to be a kind middle-aged woman. He noticed a look upon her face unlike the others but as if she knew exactly what he was searching for. Mrs. Hamlet, a middle-aged woman from the eastside who had come to the Emergency Room due to the terrible pain she was feeling in her lower back, noticed the frightened look on the face of the man and instantly knew it could be only one thing which he sought. But in that moment she began to think to herself, Lord what do I do?

Mr. Jacobs began to walk over to the lady who appeared to be in great pain, trying hard to remove the intense look that had gripped his face and replace it with a soft and gentle smile. As he came closer Mrs. Hamlet's heart began to beat faster, not out of fear of the man but out of concern as to what she should say. She noticed the intense look on the man's face had been replaced with a gentle smile but still could see the fear which he tried to conceal but continued to find a way to peek from behind the smile. 'Hello ma'am. I am very sorry to disturb you for I see you are in great pain but by any chance did you see a wallet on the floor here when you arrived this morning?'

He would be a kind and thoughtful person, thought Mrs. Hamlet. 'Mmmnnn,' groaned the woman as her pain intensified as she tried to reposition herself to speak, 'sorry… mmm… but I did not. Did you go and ask the gentlemen behind the counter if anyone turned one in?'

'Yes ma'am but he told me no.'

God what do I do, she thought as she looked to her left at a young man who had been staring at her the entire time as if he was trying to apply some fear from a distance to the woman, which apparently was working. 'I am sorry to hear that and sorry I cannot help you as well.'

Receiving an uneasy feeling as if she knew more than she was letting on, but out of respect for her suffering, he simply replied, 'Yeah me to. Well thank you ma'am and once again I am sorry to disturb you but…'God what will I do he thought? 'I was heading to pay my rent and buy food for the house. My babies are hungry and I'm running out of gas with another week remaining until payday.'

Feeling very guilty now, Mrs. Hamlet softly replied, 'Ohhh, I am so sorry to hear that and I am so sorry I cannot help you.'

With a gentle smile Mr. Jacobs replied, 'No ma'am, it is I who am sorry for bothering you while you are in such great pain. I really hope you will feel better after you leave here, I will pray for your quick recovery.'

As a silent sign of despair, mixed with a touch of guilt at the thought of going to Hell, crossed her mind, Mrs. Hamlet simply replied, 'Thanks.'

Feeling much better and arriving back at her home, Mrs. Hamlet opened the door and just as she was entering the house she heard her telephone begin to ring. 'Hey girl,' she answered, noticing the number of her best friend named Denise on the caller ID, 'how was your day?'

'Oh, it was pretty good, a little slow but all in all I must say it was okay. What about you, how did things go at the clinic?'

Mrs. Hamlet began having flashbacks of her day, and seeing the man who had lost his wallet, and just as she began to speak she was suddenly overcome with a great feeling of guilt. "My day… my day was okay. It started off very painful but I have to say thanks to the Doc I am now feeling great. I also had a little drama today as well while waiting in the clinic.'

'Really… what happened?'

'Well while I was at the clinic this morning I saw a wallet on the floor and just as I was about to pick it up, the guy across from me quickly jumped to his feet and grabbed it. Since I was in so much pain I could not get to it in time so I did not see if it was the young man's wallet or not, but he said it was and I had no reason not to believe him. I noticed the wallet was very thick from all the money that was hanging out of it. I told the young man you were very lucky because that's a lot of money you almost lost. And just as I got the last word out this frightened looking man walked into the clinic searching for something and with the level of seriousness that covered his face instantly I knew it was his wallet that he was searching for.'

'Oh my, so what happened, did you tell the man the kid had his wallet?'

The guilty feeling that had came over her had began to increase as she softly replied, 'I looked at the young man sitting across from me who had picked up the wallet expecting him to speak up but instead he looked at me with the most evil of looks as if he was daring me to say something. So I told the man I did not see it. I felt so bad for him too but, hey, what was I going to do?'

The Adulterer and the Witnesses

Smiling and walking with a sense of purpose, Brother Terrence makes his way over to John. 'Hey Brother J how are you today?'

'I am well Brother. So what did you think of today's service?'

'I must say the service today was great I was really moved by the pastor's speech.'

Nodding his head in agreement, John replied, 'Yeah, I know, it was really good, especially when he was preaching accountability. I for one know we all will be held accountable for our actions'

'I know, that's right Brother J. In the end we will have no one to blame but ourselves when we stand before the Father."

In walks Joey with a smile on his face as if he guards a great secret. "Brothers how are you both doing?'

Obviously not as good as you with that big smile on your face, John thought to himself.

'Brother Joey, what's going on?' Terrence replied.

'Ohhh, nothing much, just doing my thing as usual. What are you guys up to?'

With a slight smirk, John replied, 'Well we were just standing here talking about how much we liked the service.'

'Yeah, the pastor was on it today, he was really on it… well, as much as I like hanging out with you fellows, it's time I left.'

John waved as Terrence said, 'Okay Brother Joey, be easy and take care.'

'Okay you guys, take it light as well.'

As Joey walked away, John's smile slowly transformed into a frown as he sighed, 'Brother Terrence, you know that boy has got some nerves'

(Laughter) 'Yeah, I know that's right J. You know I see that joker with a different woman every week. I don't even know when he gets time to spend at home with his wife and kids. It's always the same old thing, different day, same crap.'

Terrence thought to himself, yeah I know, it must be nice getting to enjoy such a life.

Angry at the thought John replies, 'His day will come.'

'Well, it must be nice. My wife has me on a short leash, and when I say short, I mean short. That thing only reaches to work, church, the living room, bathroom and kitchen.'

They both begin to laugh, as John once again loosens up, replying, 'Boy you are a fool.'

'Fool nothing. I know Jenny has you on an even shorter leash!'

'You had to go there huh, you had to go there,' (Laughter)

'Hello Brothers, did one of you see my man?'

(Terrence) 'Oh, hey Sister Thelma. Yeah, Joey was just here I think he went around back.'

'Oh, okay well you both take care now and have a good evening.'

(John) 'Okay now, we'll do that and you enjoy yourself too.'

'Brother J, do you ever feel guilty knowing he is running around with all these different ladies, cheating on Sister Thelma?'

'Hey, far as I am concerned it's none of my business and I did not see a thing.'

'I hear you. It's just sometimes I think we should at least talk to the Brother.'

'Talk about what, borrowing his little black book for the weekend?' (Laughter)

The Tilting of the Scales

Now I know you are thinking each one of those stories sounds very familiar along with the actions they have chosen to take. And I know you are thinking in those moments, thank goodness for our blinkers for I see no evil. Well I am here to tell you that each of these stories has a cause and effect as to everything else in our life we encounter. Also, each of these stories possesses negative energies and since the actions were also negative in nature the cause and effects of these stories will continue to grow out of control. And they will continue to grow until what was once negative energies in someone else's world now has outgrown their world and crossed over into your world as well.

You know that for every action there will be a reaction and for every cause there will be an effect. And karma cannot be manipulated when it comes to serving its specialty to all who were directly or indirectly involved with the negative actions and or causes. Each individual will also reap their share of the negative reactions and or effects. This negative energy will continue to grow until it has consumed all the space or until it is cancelled out by the light which is the positive energy.

We often go through life with our blinkers on claiming to see no evil, not knowing that this is exactly what the Corporation wants us to do, and they know we will not disappoint them. Somewhere down the line we have begun to care more about ourselves and that of our material items than our brothers and sisters, resulting in the major shift in the energies of the planet. The planet used to possess more of the positive energy of the light and now it is quickly becoming consumed by the negative energies of the darkness. Simply put, because of all our selfish, narrow-minded ways the scales of the Earth have now tilted in favour of the darkness and the world is no longer balanced. When the scales have completely tilted in favour of the darkness then the Antichrist shall reign over the Earth for we will be in the last hours. So let's go back to what may appear to be harmless acts of selfish ignorance and see how this affects us all.

A Death of a Child, Negative vs. Positive Energies

Let's take the first one where the police officer was trying to do his job to catch the killer of the innocent child who was slain in cold blood. The woman not wanting to get involved is the action or non-action which is negative energy compounded on that which was already a very negative situation. In turn, the killer goes free and realizes that if he puts fear in the hearts and minds of the rest of the neighbours then each time he commits a violent act no one will tell on him. So the next time, instead of him fearing to get caught he will perform his violent act openly in plain sight where everyone can take witness. Then he begins his terror on the community, making more threats and implanting more fear, creating more negative energies. Now the other criminals who once feared the neighbours telling realize that if it works for him then surely it will work for them. Now what was one bad guy in the neighbourhood has quickly begun to multiply. And what was once the situation of one simple woman who was more worried about her cold grits than the slain child, has now become a problem of the entire community. The cycle now continues to grow and grow, compounding more of the negative energy on top of that which was already there, until now the killers feel no fear of the law and begin to kill the innocent people of the community as well as the policemen who were there to protect them. Now, in danger and fear of losing their own lives while being underpaid, the chain reaction of negative energies continues to grow as the policemen now turn to and begin to use excessive force, taking bribes, not responding to calls or, worse, killing innocent people as well, due to overwhelming fears of being shot first.

If we took this same story from the start and the woman had simply answered the policeman honestly and informed him that she had in fact witnessed Leroy coming out of the darkness and trying to kill JT but instead killing Samantha's baby boy, the police would have gone to arrest Leroy. He would then have ended up in jail and he and the other criminals would then in turn fear the public informing the policemen of future crimes. So, in turn, they would either be very wary of doing the crime in fear of getting caught or would not commit any more crime in fear of going back to prison. The woman speaking out would have been the positive energies of the light which will supersede and overtake the negative energy of the darkness causing the scales to remain balanced. Criminal commits crime, criminal gets caught, that is balanced. But instead now, criminal commits crime and the public fears him and allows him to commit more crimes. The scales have now tilted to the favour of the negative energies which now becomes the norm and is very hard to reverse. Now what started out as wearing your blinkers out of selfish reasons has quickly turned to wearing them due to true fear and intimidation making what was once an option now your way of life. The scales are always supposed to be balanced but when the scales tilt in favour of one over the other then the balance is off and it could take a generation to regain the balance. And in the meantime the energy that holds the edge will continue to do more harm than good.

The Theft of a Neighbour's Wages

There are many forms of this negative energy as we can see in the next story with the woman and the wallet. The woman chose not to tell the man she had in fact seen his wallet on the floor and that the individual who sat across from her had picked it up, claiming it to be his. Now, although the individual who dropped the wallet may suffer a little bit due to the absence of his money, the Universe is going to take care of him, and he will be able to make payment of his bills and feed his kids. While the lady who chose to keep her mouth closed will become the receiver of the negative reactions due to her negative actions in choosing not to speak the truth. The individual who kept the wallet will also reap much more negative reactions from his actions as well. This can spin out of control in so many ways but to keep it short it could result in the woman herself getting robbed or losing her job or a large sum of money or being passed over for a pay raise or bonus. While the guy who took the wallet may begin a life of crime and mugging people for the easy money. Or while counting the money later in a different location become victim to a violent crime resulting in him being robbed or even murdered for the same money he himself had just stolen. Sure, that cause and effect may be a little over the top but the fact remains that the negative energy will continue to grow until it is scattered by the light or the space is completely consumed from the negative energy.

Wearing our blinkers can sometimes appear to be the easiest thing to do, in some cases even the safest, but to see no evil is to assist in its growth and as it grows you will also partake in the harvest, because you helped to plant the seeds and or water the crop so shall it become your harvest as well. And in the end you will reap what you sowed. Combat all negative energies with positive energies, for the negative energy is of the darkness and the positive energy is of the light and where there is light the darkness is sure to scatter. You should always love your brother and sister more than your life itself. To see no evil, takes evil, and those that are evil are not of the Father and those that keep the Father's commandment of love know the Father and the Father will know them.

I used to have this really nice job working for this great company but a few of the co-workers were filled with a lot of negative energies. In short, they were pure evil. I had witnessed them doing negative things on the job and to other co-workers. While I did not like what I was seeing, I just put my blinkers on and continued to work very hard, thinking that if I minded my own business nothing would happen to me and I would be recognized in a positive manner for all my hard work. I tried to go above and beyond what was asked of me by man but in return fell short of what was asked of me by the Spirit.

I had witnessed two different Team Leaders and the South-west Asia Regional Manager conspiring to get several of my co-workers fired or cause them to quit, whichever came first. I watched as they compiled and created negative documents and situations against my co-workers. They even went to customers whom they had befriended to ask for help in their efforts. In the end, their efforts paid off resulting in two of the co-workers quitting and the other coming up with a scheme of his own allowing him to leave while not quitting or not getting fired. Sure, in some of the cases I spoke out to the Team Leaders and the Regional Manager informing them that what they were doing was not right. My speaking out to them, although it was the right thing to do, was not enough. I failed to perform my duty to my fellow co-workers by reporting the negative actions of the Team Leaders and manager higher up the chain and or to the Human Resources Office. I can say I did the right thing but in the end I now see I was wearing my blinkers refusing to see the evil taking place.

After the three co-workers were taken care of and gotten rid of, the evil-doers then turned their time and negative energies to me. My lack of action was the cause that began the negative effects being brought upon myself. Although I was working as hard as I could and getting positive results from the customers, they still created negative documents on me just as they did my co-workers. They began to create lies, stating that I was having issues with the customers and that I was not able to get along with co-workers. They turned my refusal to sit with them and talk about the other co-workers against me by calling me a loner, stating I did not get along well with the other co-workers. The negative energies that surrounded me every day when I went to work became unbearable to the point I realized that it was time I walked away. So, in the end what I may have been able to prevent happening to my co-workers but did not, happened to me as well. So while me and my co-workers were pushed out of a great company, the evil-doers are still with the company making their large sums of money, drawing great benefits, bonuses and pay raises while they continue their evil ways.

I still have former co-workers e-mailing me about job offers as they want to walk away from the jobs as well. The three individuals who have been sending me the e-mails all have the same thing in common with each other. They were all wearing their blinkers just as I was and although every single one of us had the opportunity to go higher or even to the Human Resources Office when we had witnessed the negative acts to our co-workers, we chose instead to stay in our own lanes, and allowed the negative energy to continue to grow in the South-west Asia Region of that company.

The company itself is not completely blameless as it knows of the negative acts as well and they continue to hide the fact and support the individual who is committing these acts. Pretty soon if not already the scales will tilt in the favour of the negative energies which will result in the company itself reaping much of the negative reactions and or effects of their harvest. It has already begun, as a lot of the individuals that are choosing to walk away are some of their brightest and hardest workers. And it will continue to grow resulting in possible law suits or, worse, some destructive individual walking into work some day and killing their co-worker just before killing themselves.

Although I took some of the negative effects from not going higher up the leadership to report what was going on, I still found favour in going directly to the wrongdoers, putting my job on the line for those who were wronged and performing my work above the standards day in and day out, continuing to spread the positive energy of the light in spite of all the negativity surrounding me on a daily basis. Because I myself was the victim of the negative energy as a direct result of placing others before myself and handling it only with positive energy, the Universe has countered the negative energies with positive energies, giving me a new job of equal pay and better opportunities. I was rewarded in the end all because I had removed the blinkers and saw the evil and confronted it face to face.

What I had learned from it all is something I have already known which is we are all connected and what happens to one of us will eventually find its way to the other. And when it happens there will be no labels to mark each negative or positive effect whereby we would know that the bad things occurring in our lives at that moment were in some way linked to something we did or did not do in the past. Although you may see no evil, just be aware that someday it may sneak up behind you and when it does your sense of feeling will not let you down as you will definitely feel it.

Chapter Fourteen:
The Teen Manipulation

Everywhere you look you will find the televisions, video games, the movies, and the life of power, fame, and fortune. The force is great, it creates these false truths that we all can be rich and famous. We look to these rich and famous people as if they are role models and great examples to look up to, and why not. They are on television, in the newspapers, the movies and, for crying out loud, they even have their own video games so it must be true. They have the fast life of men, women, and drugs; they get away with crimes that the rest of us would get arrested for. They have the beautiful women and the handsome men, they appear to be happy and straight in the moments we see their nice image cross the television or movie screens. We see them on *S-span* and *C-span*, on the News speaking with such knowledge and power and what appears to be compassion for their fellow man or constituents. We see them soaring high above their fellow athletes or speeding past them on the track and in the water. We see them with their cigarettes, tattoos and alcohol. We hear them with their music, cursing and bragging, and while alone we think, I want to be like him or her when I grow up. Role model?

Let's see, what is a role model? Well in my words a role model is a person who is looked up to as an example of how someone else would like to be. They are a person that others try so desperately to be like when actually it is that which is, but cannot truly be, but exists only in the minds and hearts of the individuals trying to emulate the one they deem to be worthy. While the individuals are not trying to live for others but for themselves. To exist for another would be fraud, and to be a fraud is a lie and a lie may require a touch of the truth to be believable but still is not the truth, nor of the truth for the truth is the truth and the lie is still only a lie. And the lie here is the belief that one man or woman is another individual's role model.

All of these images of man's greatness is the great manipulation of the teenage mind which will surely carry on to their adulthood. This is the single force which is sending you straight to the Great Prison Without Walls or Bars, only later to be transferred to the gates of hell. The serpent is a wise one, he knows the world of the spirits as well as those of the scripture. He is a master of manipulation, and he knows how to use that which we know to be truths against us making them untruths in nature. They call it role model. I call it idolizing man. I call it the Corporation's greatest weapon, their best kept secret, their trusted collectors. It's time we rescued our teens from this great manipulation, and set them back on the proper path in life.

Am I saying they cannot reach for the stars and that it is wrong to want to be all that is listed above? No, I am not, for I would be the first to tell you to follow your dreams and chase them with all your heart. For your dreams are nothing more than you following your true role model. The one true role model that is perfect in every way and has provided you with the perfect example of how to be while on Earth. All the other things are merely just a gift from the Creators, which I would tell you to accept with honour. But use your gifts, not to get others to idolize you, for revenge is that of the one who is not only the most high but also the most jealous, but to help your fellow brother and sister, to make the world a better place. We should never want another to be like us but instead better than us. We all are the keepers and the builders and what we keep is the word and spirit of God. What we build is upon that which is created as to make it better for the next.

I was very athletic and later, thanks to my bother Stan, also known at that time as DJ Fresh Ice, a very good musician. But never was it a dream of mine to follow, for my dreams were a road less glamorous with an even lesser income but a path given to me by the Spirit. A path I took and followed with great honour and tried to live in the light every step of the way. I myself have fallen to the darkness as I stumbled at times, with the fraternizing and adultery, but I still kept my faith and begged for forgiveness. My case is still under review by the one true Judge himself and on that day I will stand alone and accept my judgment.

Still, I accepted the path that was given to me, and it is up to us to teach our children the truth and keep them well informed. We must break this never-ending cycle of manipulation and encourage them to seek their role model from within, for there and only there will their true role model be found. We must teach them that there is only one true example to follow and it was he that had manifested from words to flesh to walk this very Earth to be the one true example to follow, or desire to be like, for any other claiming to be the example is a lie and the truth is not in him.

"Thus I will punish the world for its evil And the wicked for their iniquity; I will also put an end to the arrogance of the proud And abase the haughtiness of the ruthless." (Isaiah 13:11)

My eldest son, who is now 17 years old, is now on the path of becoming a musician and I have the feeling he will be a great one. Whether it came to him by dream or destiny I am not sure but what I am sure of is it comes from him. I will encourage his growth in music while at the same time never relinquishing my responsibilities as his father. I will always be the voice of reason and knowledge to him until he is ready to take on the great conspiracy for himself. And although he spent much of his teenage years growing up without his dad in the home he will always know that dad is near and will be a trusted source of information until that day comes when he shall begin to receive clarification directly from the Spirit.

Although our children are commanded by the Creator himself to honour their mother and father still it is up to us to give them something worth honouring. My eldest daughter, still living in a home without her father but with her mother, remains on the right path thanks to her mother being free of the idolizing of man and well embedded in the life of Christ. I would like to think we are doing our part of protecting our teenagers from the great manipulation with all thanks to the Creators for all they are doing in making it possible.

Chapter Fifteen:
Manipulation Completion "The Elevation"

Now it's time for graduation from high school and the Corporation is excited to see what new crops have arisen from the seeds which they so carefully planted. They wait to see the results of their compilations of different forms of manipulation and the effects they had on the masses. Your children now stand at the gates leading to the great crossroads. The battle of good and evil must take a recess while your children decide which way to go on these extremely important crossroads. Although there will be many paths to choose there is only one that will be certain, and sad to say, but we would have contributed a great deal to their selection. So good or bad the parents will be held accountable for their little ones as it should be.

This crossroad is so important because it will be their elevation. They will be elevated from that of a child to that of an adult making them solely responsible for all their actions and decisions in life from this day forward.

They will now decide what type of energy and spirit they will carry forward, they will decide what life is and will be to them. They will either choose to carry forward the Spirit with them or leave it at the gates of the crossroads. They will begin to take the famous Human Free Will for a test drive, and in that moment they will feel the freedom of choice, the complications of decisions, and the hard work it takes to make them both work. They will have a mini battle within, seeing the spiritual knowledge given at birth, the manipulative knowledge received from the Corporation, and that which they received from their parents, whatever it may be. They will be left trying to sort through it all, but in the end it will come down to the seeds that were laid and the type of foundation upon which they were laid. So ask yourself, did you fertilize the soil, provide adequate water and food and, most of all, the caring attention which only a parent can give? If you have done all of that and taught them the truths about the Creators then don't worry for the arrow will fly straight and stay on course. However, if you failed to do your duty then only God know where the arrow will fly.

I currently have a son standing at the great gates of the crossroads to elevation and I see my son feels a little lost and confused as he fumbles his way around trying to find his path. Even though I see the struggle I am careful to let him fight his way out of the egg, so once he has emerged to the other side the struggle would have given him the needed strength and confidence to carry forward with him on his journeys. I have great confidence in him for I have seen the promise in him and the promise was good. When I look at my son I see someone who may feel lost at the moment, but I also see and witness the compassion he has shown to others, the love he carries forward in his heart, the fairness which he brings to the table when dealing with others and it makes me proud that he is my son. Although I will always be the parent running and hiding behind the bushes as I set him loose to walk to the bus stop alone for the first time, still I will respect the fact that his mistakes in life will be his to make. I will forever be his true guardian standing tall, watching over him, for divided we will never be. I will always be the father and he the son and as God has never forsaken his Son even when he thought his Father had, nor will I forsake my son although there may be times when he will think differently.

This is my son I send out into the world, he is of my blood and soul so failing is not an option. He will carry with him the greatest weapon that is feared by the wicked but well received by the just. So to his enemies I say be warned and be worried for if you become his enemy then not only will you make one new enemy but instead you will make two. And to his friends, rejoice for a friend of my son will be as a son or daughter to me, for he is my son and I am connected but not in the physical realm but within the realm that matters most. And we both are children of the Creators who will choose the path of righteousness.

"Our actions will show that we belong to the truth, so we will be confident when we stand before God." (1 John 3:19)

Chapter Sixteen:
Emotions

Within our emotions there are large amounts of energy and as in all things this energy exists in two forms which are positive and negative. The positive energy is of the light, while the negative energy is of the darkness. Both energies exert great power over the physical realm and all that is in it. Every emotion we feel in life is felt by another, as we are all connected. Which is why when someone means you harm you always get an uneasy feeling even though you don't know why or where the feeling is coming from. At least in most cases because there are times when you can feel when things are not quite right and the negativity is obvious. The same goes with the positive energy. One well-placed smile could be all that is needed to brighten someone else's otherwise gloomy day. We are affected by other individual's energies everyday when we are near them. What you have to be careful of is how you redirect such energy. Will you be the type to take the negative energy and multiply it into even more negative energy? Or will you be the individual to deflect or convert that negative energy and turn it into positive energy? Well, I believe that if you are reading this book then you are the person who will not only send out the positive energy but you will absorb the negative energy only to send it back out as positive energy.

For those of you who just don't know then this would be for you, because I can relate to those of you who receive the high volume of negative energies on a daily basis until it begins to tear away at you and you feel you are just beaten down to the point you feel like a whipped puppy. Believe me, I know after 21 years in the military and another 3 as a civilian contractor working overseas. I am here to tell you I can feel your pain but all is not lost. I will give you some simple formulas for dealing with the spiritual energies in the physical realm. The formulas are as follows: (P+P=P), (N+N=N), (P+N=P), (N+P=P). Since we are dealing with energies of the spiritual realm and the positive energy is being of the light as the negative is of the darkness, the positive energy will always disperse the negative energy, for where there is light the darkness will scatter.

I have had many individuals apply their negative energies towards me up to the point I walked away from a great job. Sure, I could have stayed but it was just far too much negative energy surrounding me on a daily basis. So instead of allowing so much negative energy to dim my light I chose to walk away from a good paying job, with great benefits. Now, although many benefits was lost, I am once again smiling. Sure, there is negative energy in this job as well; still, it's on a far lesser level.

So how do we combat this negative energy? Well we do it by controlling our emotions. When the co-worker makes their attempts to ruin your name, stand fast and don't get angry and start yelling. Keep calm, keep smiling and speak softly making them aware you know what they are trying to do, while at the same time not giving into the negative sparring match. If that doesn't work, step away, get on the phone when time permits and talk to a friend or family member who can recharge you with positive energy. Just know it's okay to get angry for being angry is merely the physical emotion of how you are feeling. However, what is bad is the physical actions some choose to take after receiving the emotion. No one is telling you to be smiles twenty-four hours a day. Sometimes it's good to simply let those who carry the negative energy read the anger on your face, for that may simply be enough to ward them off. However, if you decided to add to the angry emotion shown on your face by fussing and cursing now you are feeding and watering the negative energy and it will continue to grow all over the place. Why waste your time with such negative reactions when what are you doing now is increasing the negative energy in your space as well which will surely result in you being more miserable and or stressed? That's right, the negative energy you increase in turn comes back to harm you also. As for the individual who was putting out the negative energies in the first place, they just got stronger and feel better. So your attempt to hurt them actually only gave them more strength to hurt you. Instead of getting angry try smiling and saying thank you, or simply smiling and saying nothing. Try showing them an act of kindness and always remain professional.

Negative energy is very easy to overcome, what is difficult is getting our physical self to do what it takes to overcome it. Just know that silence, smiles and kindness are some very valuable tools to have at your disposal, while shouting, cursing and hatred are all multipliers. In the end, keep the faith and know the spirits are watching over you and if, in fact, you are not the wrongdoer then the Universe will take care of you.

Chapter Seventeen:
Time

I've got time. At least that is what a lot of us choose to believe. So now I ask you a simple question, how much time do you have? How much of the time you have is guaranteed to you and in all this time you have what have you done, and what will you do with the remaining time? Very easy questions right?

Well first of all there is no guaranteed time. Each day you live is a blessing from the Creators but know this, when your time comes to end, it will not matter where you are or what you are doing, it will come. But let's take the time you think you have and break it down. I figure we use about fifty percent of our time on the planet eating, sleeping and using the bathroom, along with another twenty percent, give or take a few, going through the K-12 education system. The way I see it this leaves us about thirty percent of our life of which half of that will be spent working or driving somewhere. Now we are down to roughly ten to fifteen percent of our lifetime to do what we want. And even that is being generous, since we have not accounted for medical and dental visits, for being ill, time wasted fighting and arguing with others and so on. This is just to show you that even though in the spiritual realm time is indefinite, here in the physical realm it's not much at all. And since here in the physical realm it travels on a continuum from the past to the present continuing to the future, wasted time is something you can never get back. I know I am telling you something you already know, but the point I am trying to make to you is, sure, you have a lot of time but in the grand scheme of it all its not that much time at all.

My goal is to show you that here on Earth you really don't have much time and simply the knowledge of realizing you don't have much time will cause you to take advantage of the time you do have and not waste the little time you have sitting on the couch watching television. Enjoy your family every chance you get, go out and have some fun, find time to smile and laugh and share the gift of laughter with others. Fellowship with your brothers and sisters, do you have to go to church to do this? No you don't. Visit each other's homes, meet at the park, but no matter where you meet just the fact of socializing will be great. When not being able to do these things you quickly learn how important they are.

Find time for yourself as well, find a quiet place where you can spend time with yourself to meditate or talk to the Creators. In doing these things you will learn that time is a very valuable asset, one that is far greater in value then the world's material objects. When meditating you will find you can add many years to your life, for in the spiritual world time stands still which will allow you to take lengthy vacations within your mind and relieve the loads of negative stress from your day or week.

Find time to exercise even if you simply just walk around your home, or stretch in your living room. You don't need to do much because anything is better than nothing. Do some push-ups or sit-ups or even play with the kids or grandkids. Activity is the true fountain of youth, while being still and doing nothing strips away years from you.

"Love is patient and kind. Love is not jealous or boastful or proud. It is not rude, it is not self-seeking, it is not easily angered, it keeps no record of wrongs. Love does not delight in evil but rejoices with the truth. It always protects, always trusts, always hopes, always perseveres. Love never fails. But where there are prophecies, they will cease; where there are tongues, they will be stilled; where there is knowledge, it will pass away. Prophecy and speaking in unknown languages and special knowledge will become useless. But love will last forever!" (1 Corinthians 13:4-8)

Chapter Eighteen:
The Great Lock Down

After twenty plus years of living it happens. We are all locked away, they have succeeded in their attempt to gain control of the world population through manipulation, redirection and misdirection. And their most important success was the stripping away of our imaginations. Everyone is now on autopilot going along in the system as if there is nothing wrong, as we are all brainwashed into thinking the world is okay even though we can see and feel differently. Our compassion level is shrinking until one day there will not be any left. The love for our fellow human beings is being replaced by hate and resentment.

There is an old saying when you are in a physical prison or restraint which says, you can imprison my body but you can never imprison my mind. This means they can find freedom in their mind. Well the Corporation must have been listening because they realize that. Why imprison the body when it's the mind which controls the freedom? So now we are all held prisoners of the spiritual world, for our true freedoms were love, compassion, imagination and fellowshipping with our brothers and sisters. Now it seems that the Corporation creates one of their many slogans to cause disruption in the natural order of things, better known as order out of chaos, their slogan being "getting ahead" which translates to, do whatever it takes to get ahead of your fellow humans. So now what we have is everyone running around trying to outdo each other and talking about one another trying to make the next person look bad in order to make themselves look good. Because you are in this prison that is set up to make you think you must be better than the next man or you will be nothing.

Then they add their next slogan, "only the strong survive" or "survival of the fittest", now making you think it is okay to go after your fellow human beings. The manipulation just continues to grow until we are all fully brainwashed and when you do wrong to others you simply state, well it's the survival of the fittest. Whatever happened to the love and where did it all go? Where have the compassion and the will to help one another gone? I will tell you where it went for it did not go far, it is simply the part of us they have imprisoned. They introduced the drugs, alcohol, racism, terrorism, and all the other additional fears into the system and now you have the perfect prison that they will continue to use to control the world populations.

Most people are under the impression that it's the world's economies they are after when in all actuality controlling the world economies is merely a tool they use to gain control over what they really want and that is the soul of every living creature of this world and the next.

There is a way to take back our freedom, for our freedom is not a reality but instead it's our lost birthright which was stripped away from us all. To regain our future we must learn to see past our difference, and stand in one voice. We must learn to love and show compassion to our fellow beings. We have to remember that we all are only parts of the whole and there are no individual truths but instead just one truth which can only be found in the Spirit. No man can give you the truth for the truth has already been given to every living soul in this world and the next and it's up to each and every one of us to regain control of our minds and souls and break free. So you may ask, where do we start? And I say to you love, that is the greatest power on Earth which seems to make it the perfect starting point. For it's love which binds us all to the Creators and keeps us connected and free. This is why when they imprisoned your body your mind still found freedom. For when they imprisoned you they stripped you of all the worldly materials resulting in a stronger connection in the spiritual realm and then to the Creators themselves. Once that connection was established it was they who freed you from your physical bonds by way of the spiritual realm. This is why the mind was so important for the Corporation to gain control over for if you imprison that and strip away the love, then they have succeeded in stripping away our connection to the spiritual realm and eventually the Holy Spirit.

So forget all that you learned from their manipulative slogans such as, "all is fair in love and war" and remember that which you have inherited. Remember the example that was sent for us all to follow, remember the new commandment that was handed down to us, remember we are all part of the whole and remember that the Creators are merciful and forgiving. In case you don't remember then here is a start, for that which you inherited at birth is all the knowledge of the Universe and the one truth to all the knowledge is that God himself is love so to love one another is to love and be connected to the Creators.

The example we were sent to follow was the Word that was made man whose name was Jesus and is the Son of the Father sent to die for all our sins to be forgiven. In short, it was the greatest example of unconditional love. The new commandment was the commandment to love each other so much that you would lay down your life for each other. And as for the whole of which we are a part, that is the "Body of Christ" for no one part is more important than the next, for each part completes the whole. There is one truth in all the truths and that truth is it will be the love for each other that will set us free.

Chapter Nineteen:
"The Invisible Prison"

It's time to bring the invisible walls down. The prison is a self-imprisonment system, there is no one shackling you and throwing you in this prison. This prison is based on the "Free Will" of man therefore just as they don't throw you in it God doesn't break you out of it. You see through the lies but choose to ignore them, but from this day don't ignore them any more. Stand up for your brothers and sisters, let your voice be heard, don't settle for the lies any more. Learn how to voice your belief, for words without action are useless. Stop fighting over what they want you to fight over and fight over what is right. It's time the walls came down and you stopped letting the world and the Corporation control you. It us who should be controlling them. You would whine and complain about cable prices, airline prices, sports event prices going up. Well, here is an idea that may help, get up a petition telling them either prices go down or we'll stop buying their products. If the prices don't go down, get on the radios, in the newspapers, or on television and appeal to your brothers and sisters that this is not acceptable any more. And put some positive actions behind the words and stop buying the ticket. If the cable and satellite prices continue to rise don't buy them, give them back. They are not a necessity anyway. If the banks drive up your interest rates and carry your homes at values far less than that which you owe, then give it back. Let them have the home, walk away. Let them know you are tired and you will not accept it any more. United we stand shall become the slogan, and do it in the name of love for one another. While we are fighting about all the issues they are still screwing us all. Where are the fights and the arguments over the homeless? Where is the real fight over universal healthcare? It's time we started putting love back in the forefront. We will stand united and fight for foolishness but stand divided and fight each other over the issues that affect us all. You are blinded by the lies, remove your blinkers and see the light. Get out of the darkness for there the temperature is set to cold. It's time we took back our birthrights and got out of the house and talked to our neighbours. I once lived in a place for two years and never knew my neighbours. They would only say hello once I initiated the greeting and nothing else followed. I say again, it is time to bring the prison walls down.

One-World Government is not the answer but instead, One World United in Love is the key. For the love of my brothers and sisters everywhere from all walks of life, I write this for us all. Even though I am writing this I am afraid it is too late, the spiritual walls have been built and over the years we have come to accept it as a way of life. And as the generations pass, it has become engraved into our minds that this is the way it should be. Now they are installing the physical monitoring devices which are everywhere from one country to the next, over the highways, inside the buildings, all around the outside of the buildings, in your computers, automated teller machines and, without you knowing, inside your televisions. They're installing their cameras, scanners, radio frequency identification scanners and their great eye in the sky, the New World Order space station. Your phones, e-mails, and internet movements are already being monitored with their super-intelligent computers. They have now begun their transition from that of the unseen to that which we all see and dismiss as technology advancement. Next to come will be the implanting of radio frequency identification chips or tags into the right hand or forehead as forewarned in the Book of Revelation.

The invisible prison is completed, now to phase two, the transitioning from the invisible prison of the spiritual realm to the imprisoning of the entire world population in the physical realm. These things have been written so will they come to pass. It may be too late to stop it but not to choose sides, for our victory has been written as well as their defeat. Free your mind, heart and soul, with the one and only key to the invisible prison. The key which you inherited at birth, the one that bonds us all and, most important of all, the one that connects us to the Creators. This all-powerful key is Love. Love thy neighbours, for the world is your neighbourhood, as they are also your brothers and sisters for the Creators are our Father who art in heaven, holy be thy name, thy kingdom come, it shall be done on Earth as it is in Heaven.

Chapter Twenty:
The Prison Politics

The Scales

The scales represents the balance in all things. We always use the phrase, "that wasn't fair", or "they treat some people one way and others another". Each time you hear of differences in the way people are treated or you yourself are treated it means that the balance is off. If you see the Lady Justice you will see that even while she is blindfolded she is still holding a scale. And I am thinking, they want us to think she is blind to discrimination of any form and trying to claim she sees everyone equally and fairly and the only thing that matters is the evidence which will all be weighted equally. However, I find a flaw in her logic and I am sure the hundreds of thousands of innocent individuals all over the world who have been wrongfully imprisoned will also disagree. I believe she is blindfolded because she is saying she doesn't need to see your justice for there is only her justice, and the scale represents the balance between good and evil, which the Corporation is always actively trying to tilt in their favour.

"Evil men do not understand justice, But those who seek the LORD understand all things." (Proverbs 28:5)

The Big Party

The world parties and governments, what is this? Is it really of the people for the people and by the people? Really, what is this? Are we truly at odds with anyone or is it just merely an in-house competition for the top spot? I look at the different parties with which we are supposed to be at odds and it looks like many different little science experiments competing to see who gets to represent the school, in this case the world. It's also a form of control.

For instance, take our party system which is absolutely broken. The founders with the positive energy did not want to have anything to do with a multiparty system, in fear of dividing the nation. The founders with the negative energy did not want to have anything to do with a single government system that would simply represent the people, fearing it would give the people too much power and too much say. Now what do we have? A multiparty system that has been manipulating the public ever since its creation. It was just a master plan devised to divide and control us. Most of us proudly claim one party over the other not knowing they were designed specifically demographically based with the intent of keeping us from speaking in one voice. So while we fight amongst ourselves they are opposing us all. If you look at the parties and see what type of individuals cling to what party it would break your heart. Then to see the party implants plastered all over the television misleading and lying to the public, while some of the more ignorant individuals soak it all up. This is something that is too late to change as they have mastered this art of deception on a global scale. I will just tell you we have a government system made to look like a multiparty system and while you are being simple-minded and fighting each other they are having their lunches and dinners together, laughing at us all. So while you are feeling good because you have a party that represent your own ignorant views, just look at how much good has actually happened for the people in comparison to nothing happening at all, with the exception of throwing us ignorant folks some crumbs every now and then.

If you think I am joking, in the end look at the mess of a health care bill we will receive when it's all said and done. I will tell you when it's over the health care industry will get richer and the party people will just get suckered. For when the crying begins about not being able to afford health care and having no way to pay medical bills, the tears will know no party for we all will suffer alike. The insurance companies will smile, our government will pat themselves on the back and the people will continue to suffer. The same applies to the banks, mortgage loans, investments, and the ingenious scheme of controlling us even after we pay off our homes, the HOAs also known as the Home Owners Associations. I have a home that has a HOA and I am telling you as soon I get back from Afghanistan I am selling it. Why would you pay someone to control your home and property after paying on it most of your adult life? We have let them divide us so much that we will just sign over our house and land just to try to control our neighbours. Well, you will see someday that there is more to the HOAs than it appears and when they start to raise their fees out of the reach of most you will watch in horror as they take your home that you worked hard your whole life paying off. And I will say to you, congratulations for at least your neighbour's grass was cut.

Chapter Twenty-One:
Look to the Future

"For the revelation awaits an appointed time; it speaks of the end and will not prove false. Though it linger, wait for it; it will certainly come and will not delay." (Habakkuk 2:3)

I think it's time to take this back to the future because I think we all should know what to expect for it has been written and it has already started to come to pass. Please allow me to say once more this is just my own understanding, I don't claim to be psychic and able to see into the future nor do I claim to be a prophet with the gift of prophesy because I am neither. I am simply a man who has read the book that reveals the things to come, and I have learned some history and watched the News seeing things as they unfold. I believe my understandings, for who better to believe, the liars of the world or the voice of conscious from within me that is of the truth and from the truth.

"To one person the Spirit gives the ability to give wise advice; to another the same Spirit gives a message of special knowledge to

another faith by the same Spirit, to another gifts of healing by that one Spirit." (1 Corinthians 12:8-9)

Here is how I see things unfolding. The One-World Government will come to pass and the Body Of Corporate will have their time to rule. How and when will this happen? The how is simple because we allowed it with our hatred, bias and ignorance, failing to follow one simple commandment which is to love each other unconditionally, so much that we would give our life for each other. The when is a little more complicated and at the same time very simple as well. The when will be in the last hours before the return of the Creators themselves. Unfortunately, that exact hour is unknown to all. Even the Son, the Light and the Holy Spirit have not the hour, for even time itself is left without knowledge of the hour for God will come like a thief in the night making his arrival unknown to the Body of Corporate. So, if the exact hour is unknown then how can you know when the last hours are near? Well, we are now in the last hours, the last days and you can tell by the signs. If you don't know the signs then I would suggest you get a bible and read the book that reveals all that will come and then pray for understanding. If you have understanding and read the world signs you will see we are now in the last days. The signs are simple and clear and in no specific order. Please allow me to share my understanding as I see things happening in the near and not so near future:

A New World Order

"But woe to the earth and the sea, because the devil has gone down to you! He is filled with fury, because he knows that his time is short." (Revelation 12:12)

Since we will go to a One-World Government which is the true "New World Order", there will have to be major shifts in the global economies and power structures. There will be major shifts in borders until each continent has no borders and becomes one state. Wars that have already begun will play out until borders have been redefined and eventually completely done away with. What once were individual governments will become representative positions as the continents will fall under a one-leader rule who will have come from the Body of Corporate. As this is taking place so is the major economic and currencies shift. Riots, outrage, famine on a world scale, depressions and wars will rage until one will come forward with a way to resolve these major issues. Simply, he will say, 'Let's unite as one, and this union will bring peace, for how can you have war with no opposing forces? The sharing of the world food supply will end hunger around the world.'

Our false utopia will now have been created.

One Currency

There will be another major shift in currencies. As the Euro was created, so shall there be one form of currency for the Americas, as Mexican, North American and Canadian borders open. This type of shift will also happen in the Asian countries and then also the African countries. This will happen until every continent is operating on one currency. Then major economies will begin to fall as the great depression will hit. The Body of Corporate would have already secretly created a new form of banking system off-shore from any of the major continents. They will say the cause of the unstable world currencies was due to counterfeit bills and suggest we go to a more secure form of currency, resulting in the end to all cash as we know it as it will become a micro-bio-chip on a card. This chip will be state-of-the-art, it will have the ability to hold more data then the best home computer on the market today. This chip will hold all your personal information, along with all your debt, investments and finances. This will become your universal card. In other words there will be no need for all the others such as driver's licence, voting cards, credit cards, identification cards, debit cards, or any other cards. It will be encoded with your DNA as well. Little known to you, it will also be encoded with a radio frequency chip and GPS chips as well.

Next they will tell you identities are being stolen, that the criminals have figured out a way to use your bio-cards and steal your identities, so they will be offering you a safer alternative. They will tell you how the countries of France, Dubai and China have been using this technology of implanting a chip in their hands and begin to offer you this as an option. At first it will be on volunteer basis, and then later mandatory, to receive it on either your right hand or forehead. Once you have been implanted I will tell you now you would have officially received the "Mark of the Beast". In other word you will no longer be the Lamb of Our Shepherd but instead you would have become branded as the cattle of the Body of Corporate.

"He also forced everyone, small and great, rich and poor, free and slave, to receive a mark on his right hand or on his forehead." (Revelation 13:16)

Religion

Religious freedoms will become a thing of the past. In short this will be the thing war is waged over. Countries will start demanding that their citizens be of one religion, and those that oppose the change will first be given the opportunity to convert or leave. Those who choose to stay will be jailed, then it will elevate to their termination. The war over the different religious holy locations will start to take place. When it comes to signs, this will be one of the most important. For the day will come when the rebuilding of King Solomon's Temple for the third time, which will also be named "The Third Temple", will take place. King Solomon's Temple, also called "The First Temple", "The House of That Which is Holy", "Sulaiman" to the Muslims and "Jerusalem Temple" to the Jewish, was built in Jerusalem on the hill of Mount Moriah, also known as the "Temple Mount", in 960BCE. It was destroyed by the Babylonians in 586BCE, then rebuilt in the same location. The Second Temple stood from 516BCE to 70CE and again it was destroyed, only this time by the Romans.

The "Word" has foretold there will be a Third Temple rebuilt once again on Mount Moriah in Jerusalem, and when this takes place we will know the last hours draw near. Currently, "The Mosque", also known as "The Dome of the Rock" and in Arabic as "Qubbat As-Sakhrah", which happens to be the third holiest site of Islam following only behind Mecca and

Medina occupies this site since its construction between 684-691CE. This site is holy to both Jews and Muslims. The Jews believe it was the site where God himself stopped Abraham from sacrificing his son Isaac, while some of the Christian faith also believe that the Spirit of God himself once presided in the Temple. The Muslim believes this is the place where the Prophet Mohammed rose to Heaven. This will be the reason for the unrest and great conflicts in the region during the last days.

Surveillance Technology

You will begin to notice all kinds of advancements made in the technological world of surveillance. There will be cameras on every street in every country, provinces, cities, towns and later every neighbourhood. They will be accompanied by other devices such as radio frequency identification hubs or scanners, more elaborate GPS and cellphone towers, and facial recognition devices loaded with the latest and greatest facial enhancement and recognition software. Cameras will be inserted in every computer, cellphone, landline phone, GPS system, television, automatic teller machine, gas pump, vehicle, place of business, traffic light, underpass, overpass and automobile. All lines will become one, turning the home phones, televisions and computers into one interchangeable item linked directly to you. At first in your home then later anywhere you may go.

Claims will be made of high thefts which will prompt them to add radio frequency identification chips in everything from your clothes, shoes and bags to your home appliances. Once the great Mesh System is in place there will be nowhere on Earth you will be able to hide from the hundreds of thousands of land-based cameras, and cameras they have in space. They will all be controlled by satellites and capable of being controlled and run from their new state-of-the-art control centre or international space station.

Chapter Twenty-Two:
Selecting Your Cell Mate

When two becomes one is a beautiful thing, although sometimes it may not appear so. There is a way whereby both man and woman can have their happily ever after, all it requires is for them to learn the major factors of human nature when dealing with the two. Why must we learn to live and, better yet, why must we live to learn? Most of us are not living according plan. Some of us are just shooting from the hip and in the end we will all account for our works. Some of us have forgotten how to live due to the manipulations and misdirection inserted into our lives by the Corporation and our mortal enemies. Sometimes we simply get disoriented and lose our way.

There are a lot of things that can cause us to lose focus so I will simply go back to the original distraction that caused sin to fall on us all, which was our very selves, both man and woman. We are the biggest distraction to each other and our number one cause for sin. There was no accident in the way both man and woman were created. While man was made of bulk and of muscles, woman was made with a little more fat under the skin for a softer look. While it is clear the most natural reasons for the differences is for us to mate and fill the earth with our species, it is sometimes unclear what the selection process is. A lot of us get ahead of the game and begin to mate long before the vows are made. And to add to it, we may do it with several different mates that we never intend to marry. Even though it is now too late I must admit I wish not only that I had waited but I had waited for the right woman who I was destined to be with.

There are several ways you will know when the woman is the right one and they are through our own selection process, through a vision sent by the Holy Spirit, and the spontaneous reaction, better known as love at first sight.

The Selection Process of Man

I will start with the selection process because even after the other two processes have happened if she was Mrs. Right these things will still apply. When going through the selection process you have heard the old saying that looks don't matter. Well nothing could be further from the truth, especially when it comes to the man. Now to understand this statement you must first understand the human nature of both male and female.

The man is a creature that was created with the most mass and built so as to show we are the "Beast" of the humanoids. It's clear that our original purpose was to work the fields, fertilize the eggs and protect the household. Being the beast we are drawn to all beauty, for without this trait there will be no certain pull to the woman which is a mechanism for ensuring the survival of the species. Since we are the brawn instead of the brains, sexual relations is our encoded priority, which means sex becomes a high priority to man. Having this encoded as a priority sets us up for cause and effect, governed by the amount of sex that is received and the level of intimacy.

So first, let's talk about the selection process and the fact that looks really do matter. Male as a mind-based creature means that for him to enjoy anything he must be able to see it in his mind as looking good. It has nothing to do with the functionality of the object, more so the looks. For instance, when a man goes looking for a car the first thing he looks for is the outside appearance. For if that car accelerates from zero to eighty in five seconds, gets sixty miles to a gallon and never needs an oil change but looks ugly, it might as well be a *Pinto* because the male will leave it right there on the car lot. When looking for anything, the first thing we will look for is the looks, so why should it be any different when looking for a mate?

Well, regardless of what anyone says, it's not. When looking for a mate you must be very careful. First of all every man has an exact measurement of the woman's body he is attracted to. The moment a man spots a woman his mind's eye has already performed the calculations and determined whether further examination is warranted or if it's just a look and go. Now what I am talking about has nothing to do with lust because, as I said, man is the beast with the sexual appetite. This means most men will do almost any woman, but that is lust and fornication, it has nothing to do with love and marriage, so stay with me. Once the man has established the physical aspects of the body size and shape are in order, it is time to get a little more specific. So next he will check out the face which again will be instantly recognized as beautiful or do-able. He will subconsciously examine every feature of the face from her hair, forehead, eyes, nose, lips, ears and facial hair. At this time the skin and skin tone are examined and it will register with him if the woman is beautiful or a match to him. Where some men go wrong is they see features they don't like and still try to make it work, but I tell you that marriage will be destined to fail. Next, the man will go down to the woman's breasts. Every male has a breast size that is perfect to him and to him only. So women, if you are out there committing fraud with the fake bras and fake rubber butts, you better find a way to let him know the real size of those areas as soon as possible. Am I saying lift your shirts up on the first day and expose yourself to a stranger? No, I am not, I am saying do it on the second date. Yes ladies, I was just joking! But the way you can do it is if you feel you really like this guy then maybe the next date wear a normal bra and panties that will show your real size. Trust me ladies, this will save you a lot of heartache in the future. The man needs to make sure the breast size is exactly to his liking.

Then he will need to feel your touch and touch your skin. This is why both male and female go through a little playful moment when they are courting and begin touching and bumping into each other. Then there is the smell. That's right, man must find the woman whose smell is pleasant to him. Each woman gives off a chemical reaction when courting and a man picks up on it subconsciously. Sure, your cosmetic smell is important as well but not as much as this natural odour.

You can say what you want to say, but if this process of selecting the exact woman is ignored there will be effects. The reason the man must go through this process is because if he has selected his woman tailor-made to his liking then no matter if ten, twenty or hundred years pass he will still stare at his mate as if she was the only woman on the planet. He will always be into her and she will feel it, which is very important to the woman as you will see in the woman selection process.

Ladies, this cause will have lots of effects such as the man will want more sex with you as well which could be a problem but a good thing as well, as we will discuss in further detail later.

The Selection Process of Woman

The selection process of a woman is far different from that of a man, for the woman who has been carefully sculpted to be an attraction to man is noticeably much smaller in build, much softer and smoother to the touch with less muscles. It is clear the woman is the "Beauty" of the humanoids and also built for thinking, making her the brains as well. Sorry guys, I promise I am not the male basher but the truth is the truth. All the true knowledge in its purest forms has come by way of "Woman". After all, wasn't she the first to bite from the "Tree of Knowledge" which means from the time she took her bite till the time she convinced "Man" to follow, "Woman" was the first to become educated and was the smartest human being in the entire Universe. It was through "Woman" that "Man" found true knowledge.

Since the woman is the brains of the two and already possesses the beauty, then looks are not so much of a priority as it is with man. While man has to go into great detail in selecting a woman, all a woman needs is one look and she can select a mate for life. What the woman is looking for is not in the details but more so the structure. For instance, whereas the man is the brawn, the worker, the mater and protector the woman is hard-coded to look for and recognize these traits. While the male wants to mate to ensure the survival of the species, the woman wants to nourish and protect the offsprings to ensure their survival. The woman must be the thinker, for her role is to provide basic nourishment of the body and the mind for that which she loves, protection and security from the environment, and comfort.

When a woman looks for a mate, although she is looking for looks as well, the looks are just not as high on the priority list as they are for man. That's why when a woman looks at a man for the first time she will know right off if she will take the man as a mate. She is looking first to see if that man is capable of providing protection for her and the offsprings, if he is solid enough to perform the proper labour to place food on the table. Then she looks for the everlasting look in his eyes of being taken with her which will provide her with the feeling of security that the man will stick around.

If you doubt this process let's go back to the car. When a woman sees that same ugly car, at first she may think, what an ugly little car. But once the dealer informs her that the car is very reliable, that she will get sixty miles to the gallon, never have to change the oil and if it breaks down they will repair it for free, that's it. Man will, of course, be unhappy because they are driving the ugly little car off the lot that day. But while the man will pout and always see the ugly little car, the woman will simply smile and learn to love the ugly little car which to her has now become the cute, reliable little car.

Don't feel sorry for man, for the woman, the brains of the marriage, will see his unhappiness and will allow him to go get his nice looking car and, a year later, will also pick him up off the side of the road when he breaks down. Just joking guys, but you get my point, the woman is the thinker. Where man overreacts or reacts too quickly, a woman is more detailed and calculating. So back to the selection process. Once the woman realizes that the man who is courting her can provide the essentials she then engages back into deliberate selections of not only looks but attitude as well, for the attitudes and looks will go hand in hand with security.

The Vision

The vision is quite simple. This requires nothing of either the man or woman, for the Spirit showed you one another in a dream or thought and destiny arranged the meeting. If you have a vision of your mate I can tell you how important it is to wait till your path crosses with the lady of your dreams. I have been married twice; the first was to a woman I chose in spite of being shown my wife in my thoughts and dreams. After reading the bible I learned of the specific selection process and the detail which Jesus taught us to go into when selecting our wife and in spite of my vision I still went out and selected a woman. Well, the selection process worked physically. I was very attracted to the woman although there were some key physical aspects I overlooked, but for the most part I was still taken by her. There were times when I found myself staring at the things that did not match what I wanted but for eleven years I found myself very attracted to her physically. But mentally we were a complete mismatch which caused us to continue to clash and the only reason I feel we lasted so long was because I was always away due to my life in the military. After we got married I think we both realized it may have been a mistake because we were clashing like cats and dogs all the time. Don't get me wrong. She was a good woman, she just was not good to me nor was I to her which guaranteed our certain divorce. After our divorce I told myself I was done with women, I was just going to focus on work and making money and nothing more. Only I had forgotten all about

When I was nine or ten years old I had recurring dreams about the same woman. I knew this was not just a dream because not only was I seeing her but I saw her in great detail from every part of her face and her hair and, to really get tripped off, I even heard her voice. When I was around ten years old I and some of my friends stood at the end of my driveway when one of them brought up the subject of the perfect woman. So it turned from a conversation to one saying, describe to the group your idea of the perfect woman. Well, when my time came she was in my mind and I began to describe her in great detail from her hair, her eyes, nose and mouth to her breast size and height. I even spoke of how her voice sounded and the way she spoke in a kind of a broken English. I even told them where I thought she was from because that was the only location I have seen women that looked like her on the television. They were in awe of how I was able to describe someone I had never seen in such detail, until I told them I was seeing her in my dreams.

Once I grew up I saw a woman that had almost been perfect in my selection process. However, there were still some things that did not fit but I thought it was close enough. We eventually got married and the marriage was good in many ways, but in many ways there were a lot of signs that showed we were not a match. Nevertheless, we reached a point where we knew we could no longer coexist and decided to go our separate ways. After the final decision was made to go our separate ways I was going through a bad case of depression and I was dealing with a broken heart. It was not so much losing my ex-wife, which was in itself very hard for me, but it was more knowing I would not have my two little ones who are so dear to my heart growing up in the same house with me any more. The pain was so great I actually found myself contemplating suicide. I would go to sleep each night with lots of pills beside me on the nightstand and my windows covered with dark blankets to block out all the light. Every weekend I would do this and take more and more of the sleeping pills till one four-day weekend I slept for three days straight. And not having any friends or family there with me no one even noticed my absence. It was like the Father was telling me my time had not yet come to cross over to the other side.

Then all of a sudden the guy I was replacing started coming by the room looking for me and asking me to go out with him which I kindly turned down. I was coming off an eleven-year marriage whereby I had altogether given up clubs and not only that but I was not in the clubbing mood. Now SSG Price was very popular, he had friends so he did not need me to go out with him. In fact, he did not even know me, yet he just kept coming back every other day trying to get me to come out. The weekend after I had slept three days I realized that eventually I was going to do the unthinkable and all I could think of was my little ones and the life I would be condemning them to as well as my soul going straight to hell. So the following weekend when SSG Price came knocking, although still reluctant to go, I told him I would go. I really did not feel it but he tried his best to cheer me up as we went to a few stores and riding around town. Then once it had gotten dark he asked if I would go to a club on post with him at which time I said okay. But the moment we walked through the door I was instantly reminded why I stopped going to clubs. I had never like the smoked-filled, cramped spaces to the point in the past when I went I could not wait till the night was over and I was back in my barracks room. After five minutes he could tell I was really not into it because I did not drink, being a non-drinker, and I would not dance so he asked me if I wanted to leave at which time I said yes.

When we left the NCO club he asked if I would mind going to one more location. It was almost as if he had a mission of not letting me return to my room that night. I don't know if it was due to the constant darkness or the load of sleeping pills outside of the containers on the nightstand or both. Either way he was determined as if he was sent from God himself. So I told him I would go with him to the last location. When we walked to the other club, which was larger with room to move about, it was loaded with beautiful women and lots of drinking soldiers smoking and talking while staring at the people dancing on the dance floor. When we walked in I was looking away to scan the place and I noticed two women walking towards us and, as they got closer, the one crossed the other as if she had known SSG Price. It did not really bother me because, one, I did not want to talk and, two, I always get that type of reaction from women in the club due to my extremely young-looking appearance.

SSG Price and his friend led the way to an empty table. Once we arrived at the table I sat in the seat facing the bar instead of the dance floor while SSG Price sat directly to my front and his friend named Tina sat to his left. Her friend, whose name was Sheba, sat to my right but also seemed as if she did not prefer to sit with anyone as well. SSG Price and his friend were talking while I paid the lady next to me no attention at all. In fact, I did not even look at her once but instead my eyes were focused on a woman sitting at the bar. And I remember thinking to my myself, wow what a beautiful woman. I believe the little attention I was paying to Sheba, the lady who sat next to me, was starting to make her angry when after all she did not even want to come and meet me in the first place. She was new to the club environment herself and after arriving in country her friends were trying to take care of her. The other girls were pushing her to go with Tina when she went to meet her friend since I was with him. They wanted her to meet a friend since she was so far away from home as well, but instead she just wanted to remain in the comfort of her little corner. When she first saw me she also thought I was too young which would mean I would only have played games with her as younger guys do and she did not want any part of that. Well, she decided to go along with Tina to meet me anyway only to have me pay her no attention, but focusing on the woman at the bar instead. So she began to speak to Tina in a language I did not understand. Later, I found out she was telling her friend she was leaving because I was not paying her any attention. Tina told her to try to talk to me instead, so she did. And when she spoke I got a chill up my spine for I instantly recognized the voice with a hundred percent certainty. It was so unbelievable because the voice I heard along with the broken English accent was that of the woman from my dreams. As I sat there thinking it could not be, I slowly turned my head to see the face of this woman and that's when I just knew I had seen an angel from Heaven itself for it was her. It was the woman from my dreams. My heart began to beat as if I was about to suffer a heart attack. I quickly turned my head back towards the bar to focus once again on the woman sitting there. I was wondering, what is this, what did this mean? Was I back in my dreams and just had not woken due to the sleeping pills? What was going on, I wondered? I decided at that point to buy her a drink and then SSG Price and I decided to leave. He mistook the crazy look on my face as meaning I was ready to go, so we did.

Once we exited the club and began walking home I was still spaced out and SSG Price asked me, 'What is the matter?'

I was still walking with the thousand-mile stare when he repeated the question, 'Hey man, what's the matter, are you okay?'

That is when I told him, 'That is my wife. I mean she is going to be my wife; I mean I think we are going to get married.'

As I fumbled, trying to find the right words to explain, he said, 'Hey man, that is not how it works. You are only supposed to have fun and then you set the sparrow free.'

I replied, 'Sparrow, what sparrow? First of all I am not that guy and second of all I am serious. I have been dreaming about that woman since I was nine or ten years old and without question she will be my wife.'

I think at that point he saw the seriousness on my face and simply said, 'Okay homes, go for it.'

After that night Sheba and I would continue to meet at the club. We had our own special table in the corner away from the dance floor where we would always just sit and talk. After just the fourth time of seeing her I could not keep my secret any longer and finally told her I was in love with her and she was going to be my wife. Well, of course, she told me I was crazy in so many words. She told me, 'You've only known me for four days how can you say you love me?'

I told her, 'Easy, because I loved you from the first day I saw you', knowing then was not the time to tell her I had dreamed about her my whole life. We even went back and forth over it leading me to telling her, 'Look, I know how I feel.'

In the end I found out she had a secret of her own. Little did I know she had many dreams as well, of marrying a tall, dark-skinned man who wore the uniform of a soldier! She had three recurring dreams of getting married, to travel to a foreign country and to go on a submarine. Little did she know her dreams was telling her she would married a tall, dark man in the military and he would take her away to a foreign country. Here it is, 6 years and 6 months later since we were married and

8 years since we met, and when I look to her I stare in disbelief that she is my wife. To this day I am still very attracted to her, like I was the first day we met. So the moral of the story is the vision from God himself is the certainty, and the truth, for it is the gift from the Spirit himself.

I often credit SSG Price with saving my life and to this day every once in a while I send him an e-mail letting him know all is well and giving him thanks for saving my life. Needless to say, when the Spirit sends you a mate I can assure you he or she will meet all the specifications you desire in a mate for the Creators know what you are looking for better than you yourself. Not only was she a perfect physical match but in mind and soul as well. She possesses all the true traits of the woman, being the brains of the house, although she would argue this point saying it's me, focusing on the security, nourishment and comfort of her family. I give all praise to God for my wife.

Love at First Sight

Every once in while there comes a time when fate steps in and, just in passing on the street, in a store, college or school, your eyes will meet with another and in that instance you both know it was meant to be. True love at first sight needs no confirmation for it is of the Spirit and confirmation has been set and destiny is in agreement. However, there is also the dreaded lust out there which is not of the Spirit and therefore requires you to challenge and confirm because lust can sometimes appear to be love at first sight. However, after you take a closer look you will realize something is missing. So when in doubt simply go through your whole selection process and if one thing is off from that which you desire in a mate then it is not love at first sight but merely lust which caught your eye. You will know it to be love at first sight because everything about the other would be exactly what you were looking for in a mate, for the Spirit does not lie for it is the truth. Love at first sight is a beautiful thing, just be careful not to let it pass you by in fear of speaking to one another. When you both are acting as if you knew each other for eternity and can't take your eyes off each other, you need to seize the moment and don't be scared to approach one another. In the end if it was truly meant to be it will. However, you can still blow this one, so don't.

Chapter Twenty-Three:
Harmony Amongst Cell Mates

"The wife's body does not belong to her alone but also to her husband. In the same way, the husband's body does not belong to him alone but also to his wife." (1 Corinthians 7:4)

It is easy for two people to come together as one but staying together and living in harmony is something totally different. To do this, both individuals must know the factors of the other's human nature. In other words, the man must know the factors of the woman's nature and the woman must know the factors of the man. Now when I say factors to what am I referring? Well, I am talking about those things that play a major role in the life of both humanoids. Knowing these things can save each individual a lot of heartache and pains.

Starting with the man, most may disagree but since this is the way I see things from my own understanding then their disagreement is understandable and accepted.

When it comes to the man we are the "Beast" of the relationship with the bulk and the muscles. I see us as being the worker of the fields, the protectors while also being the attracted. Since we were built with the brawn we are not truly the thinkers of the relationship. These three things, although simple in form, are quite complicated in a relationship. Men being in the role of the attracted means we are created to be the go-getter when it comes to sexual relations with women. It also means by nature we will crave it, want it, and desire it all the time.

Now the woman factors, on the other hand, are security, protection, nourishment and comfort, while also being the attracter. They were carefully crafted to draw the man's attention, making her the "Beauty" of the relationship. And using it she will or should carefully select her mate with her factors as a priority and then consider the looks after that.

Man, being the attracted and already built for his factors, is designed to focus on the looks first and the other factors, well, they are just there. So how would knowing these things help your relationship? Well, they help on so many levels, for each factor will serve as a cause and effect in your relationship and it will be up to you to determine if it is a negative effect or a positive one. And the same goes for the cause. Just keep in mind the simple formulas we discussed under emotions because they apply here as well.

So let's take the security factor for the female. The husband must know at all times that the woman needs to feel secure, not just financially and with materiel items, because she will be the first to tell you she can get all of that herself, but instead secure in the relationship. When in a relationship she wants to feel that the relationship is strong and will never end. So how does knowing this help the man? Well, easy, because it is the signs given off by the man that trigger the feeling of security in the woman.

So now let's look at the factor of man being the attracted and into looks first. It helps the woman to know this because every time she prepares herself she must keep this in mind because once she learns about her husband she will know if he likes or dislikes make-up, if he likes her hair a certain way, or if he likes or dislikes tight closes, and so on. Now you are probably thinking, what does the male factor of liking looks first have to do with the female factor of security? Easy, it's all based on the cause and effects rule. Each person should go into the relationship being selfless and think of the other more than themselves which in the end would create a selfish-free relationship. So when the woman is not being selfish and gets dressed in the morning she will or should consider all the things her man likes and prepare accordingly.

Once she does that with her man in mind it now becomes a cause. When the man sees her this way to his liking it will cause him to stare at her, crave her and want her. He will be thinking about her all day, anticipating what may happen when he gets home, and without being known to him this is the effect. Now when the man comes home, the first thing he wants to see is his beautiful wife. He is going to want to touch, hug, hold and kiss his beautiful wife. So the effect from what the woman did earlier has now become the cause. When the woman feels such sincere desire for her and sees the deep looks in his eyes, hearing how he could not wait to get home to her, it causes her to feel secure and she is now reaping the positive effects from her own original selfless act.

That whole cause and effects situation could easily be negative if, instead, the woman piles on her make-up knowing her man hates make-up. So now, as she is leaving he doesn't fool around or stare at her, and when he gets to work he doesn't think about her. Then, when he gets home, he goes straight to the television and barely notices her. Now she is angry and feels less secure all because she chose the selfish act.

The next factor is protector. Man, you have got to stop being selfish for this is an important factor that takes place on the subconscious level of both the man and the woman. So let's take the man who knows this factor is important for the woman. Although she may never tell you that you are carrying a car tyre around your waist, keeping it to herself, inside she is feeling it and so are you. So you notice the car tyre around your waist and you decide to be selfless and think that she wants a man that she feels looks the part of a defender and not the one who gets sand kicked in his face at the beach. So you start doing your sit-ups and crunches every night before going to bed and each morning when you wake up. Now you notice the chest is starting to rise again from the push-ups and the tyre is starting to go flat and then disappear altogether from the crunches and sit-ups.

At the same time, the woman must know the male factor of being the attracted and what comes with that are the high desires for sexual relations. How do they come into cause and effect when the man performs his selfless act of working out and going from the chubby to the fit? It became the cause when the woman saw you become

Tarzan, her protector. She became excited and turned on wanting to rub and lay on your chest and in the comfort of your arms and this feeling triggered her sexual emotions, becoming the effect. Now she is ready to jump your bones and she gives you the best sexual relations of your relationship which now becomes the cause. The man is so happy and excited to be receiving the royal treatment he in turns pick it up a couple of notches himself delivering the performance of the year leaving his woman very satisfied, becoming the positive effect as you both are left very happy.

Again this could easily be a cause and effect in the negative form as well. You both notice the car tyre but the woman has become used to it and will not say a word. You, the man, see it but just don't care, even though it is drawing on your sexual energy as you don't feel very sexual any more. So now you both get set in your routines and it becomes okay when you don't have sexual relations. The man, being the attracted, wants sexual relations; the woman, not seeing her protector, wants them but is not so excited about it. The man feels the little excitement and feels self-conscious but still the craving exists. So when they come together the performance from them both is lacking passion with more of the "let's get it over quick" attitude. When this happens, more often the woman is left being the dissatisfied one as either the man is too tired or doesn't care to keep going, delivering her the unhappy ending. The woman may even fake the happy ending just to get it over with quickly. Either way, your woman is left unsatisfied. And even though you may play it off, still it will leave you feeling guilty resulting in a negative cause and effect.

The same holds true about each factor, so if you both know the other one's factors and think of the other person instead of yourself in the end you will be delivering yourself positive effects every time. The most important factor you both must remember is the sexual relations factor, for every time the partner wants it, whether it is the male or female, you must perform, and you must perform exceptionally, thinking only of the partner and not yourself.

"The husband should fulfil his wife's sexual needs, and the wife should fulfil her husband's needs." (1 Corinthians 7:3)

If you do this, the experience will always be enjoyable making each of the other factors positive causes which will result in positive effects.

When you are not able or willing to have sexual relations you both need to be in agreement. Also it would help if you come up with some alternative ways of pleasing the other. Never use the absence of sexual relations as a punishment. Even when you are angry with each other and one of the partners wants sexual relations you should still put on a performance just as good as if you were happy, if not better. If you are the type who chooses to use the absence of sexual relations as a punishment just remember this is a selfish act which in turn will become a negative cause, which would have a negative effect, triggering you to give another negative cause resulting in the partner who wants to have sexual relations with you after a fight, which was a positive, now delivering you a negative effect.

"Do not deprive each other except by mutual consent and for a time, so that you may devote yourselves to prayer. Then come together again so that Satan will not tempt you because of your lack of self-control." (1 Corinthians 7:5)

Chapter Twenty-Four:
Life Beyond The Prison Boundaries

I truly believe there are more intelligent life forms in the Universe but, to most, this cannot be for it would ruin all that they have come to believe. But in this case the truth does not hinge on one's beliefs just the facts. So either there are or there are not and I personally think there are. I just cannot believe that we are so self-absorbed where we think we can lay sole claim to intelligence, intellect, spirits and souls because we can't. We look at our sun with its different name from the other stars and we hold it dear as an original creation, the only one of its kind, when we all know they are all the same and not just one but an infinite amount. We also know that there are many moons, more moons than we can count. So why do we feel that our solar system is the only one of its kind that exists, when there is clear evidence that there are many solar systems and galaxies? Logic would say that if there are many solar systems and many different galaxies, and an endless number of stars, then why is it not safe to assume that the number of planets out there could range in the billions or trillions or, even better, countless? Now logic would also say that if there is a countless number of planets and suns, there are many possibilities of the planets being the right distance from their suns to sustain some sort of life form, whether they are humanoid or not. Their civilizations could be far more advanced than we are or vice-versa. Nevertheless, I think it would be safe to say we are not alone, and some day the rest of us will realize it.

Anyone who believes in the Son of God has this testimony in his heart. Anyone who does not believe God has made him out to be a liar, because he has not believed the testimony God has given about his Son." (1 John 5:10)

Chapter Twenty-Five:
Meet the "JUDGE"

There will come a day when we will all stand before the one true Judge and he will be the only one who will judge us for our works. If you want to find favour in his courts then I recommend you read and learn his rule book, user manual, instruction guides, technical manual or, simply put, the bible. Pray for understanding, for no man can teach you that which he has already given you in the spirit. No man in the physical form can understand the spirit of the Creators and nor can you understand the Creators while you are in the physical form. So to find the answers that you seek, return to that from where you came. Find a nice comfortable space where you can meditate or pray, and leave your mind and heart open as you go to sleep, for your dreams are not only sights and pictures but a gateway as well.

Always remember to love unconditionally all of your brothers and sisters of the world, love and trust in his Son Jesus Christ, and remember he is a merciful God so don't be afraid to ask for his forgiveness in the name of the Son. Remember these are the last hours and the Antichrist is here and they are many so be aware of what others are trying to teach you. Don't be afraid to challenge them. Ask them about Jesus for if they don't believe he is the Son of God and came to walk amongst us in the flesh and die for our sins then depart their teachings for they are not of God nor the Body of Christ, but they are of the Antichrist, the Body of Corporate.

These are the last hours, the signs are there, open your eyes for when the end comes it will be fast. Don't be afraid to take the journey, for to receive enlightenment is to receive a blessing. Many of us travel through life ignoring the Spirit, the truth and, essentially, God himself, expecting still to find favour in his courtroom. But instead of favour all that will be found is loneliness, for in the end he will remember all of those who did not remember and keep his commandments, his word, his promise, and his spirit and in the end you will call his name, and he will respond according to your works. For you did not know him a lifetime, and he will not know you in the end.

Before it's too late take them off, remove your blinkers, and look to your left and your right, reach down and help your brothers and sisters up. Don't be the one whose only defence is, I didn't know. Find your vision, calibrate your sight, and let's do what's right. Love your brothers and sisters as you love yourself because, believe me, that is exactly what you are doing. For loving others is to love yourself, and because you love in truth, you also love the Father who will respond in kind, and love you more than many lifetimes. And when there are no more lifetimes left, his love will only just have gotten started.

"This is how we know what love is: Jesus Christ laid down his life for us. And we ought to lay down our lives for our brothers." (1 John 3:16)

"No man hath seen God at any time. If we love one another, God dwelleth in us, and his love is perfected in us." (1 John 4:12)

Chapter Twenty-Six:
Words in Harmony

What Is The "Truth"?

What ever so elusive, forever ducking and hiding, escaping and sliding, dipping and diving, but still surviving, always there, but can't be found, neither in the air or sea nor on or beneath the heavens or ground-

Where, oh where can it be, you ask, as it hides in the open merely behind its mask-

Why does it run, evades and escapes, wearing its masks and hooded capes, then appearing only to again disappear is the question of the ages, the unsolvable equation, the mysteries of mysteries, and secrets of the secret, the ironic joke of destiny and poetic justice of karma, that lifelong drama, creates that which should not be but will survive all eternity-

It is a question with no answer for the answer is the

very question itself, veiled in illusions, revealed in the subconscious of dreams and death, manipulated every time it is manifested in reality which is nothing more than the opposite to me-

What is this poetic thing that has come into being, what is this question of questions, plagued by hypnotic suggestions, this evidence of life without the proof, and yet it still remains WHAT IS THE TRUTH, and the sleuth will simply say the TRUTH is the TRUTH...

What is Blinkers (Selfishness)

"It's a Gift from the Corporation Father, can I keep them?"

Oh what focus, what clarity do I see, not lateral nor backwards of me, can be seen as I crawl, walk or run, the absence of vision appears to be fun. No more bad times or sad times just only the good times I choose to see in these brand new blinkers that were given to me. Oh can they be, they have to be with a certainty the greatest gift ever given to me, I see what I want, when I want, even how I want, and after all isn't that the point-

Father, oh Father can I please keep them, I will care for them, clean them, even purchase the best of treatments for them, I will never leave home without them for this I swear, without a care, I will walk upright for sin I wouldn't dare-

My love for you is great indeed, I used to beg and plead for your sympathy and now with these I will repay your love by walking the straight and the narrow, free as a sparrow, not looking left nor right, not seeing wrong but right, for the righteous is all I will keep in my sight. As I plant your seeds and see the stem, start to grow, rubbing shoulders with the rich and ignoring the poor, buying my stocks, disregarding the charities, given well to my friends, ignoring my enemies, bypassing the homeless, but being the best, outdoing all the rest, when donating to our office going-away chest-

I will know and show it must be the results of this gem of a gift that each day I leave home with, for from the Corporation I had received but did not believe, due their greed how could something so good have been achieved, the creation of blinkers for the human race, making life so perfect eliminating the need for grace-

Father please I beg and plead I'm down on my knees, not praying but saying this must be right, keeping all of the ugliness and sin out of my sight. I am so happy I am happy indeed, for what do I need to see others in need, why must I feel their pain while their down on their luck, I've been down once before so I know it can suck, must I suffer during my bad times and theirs, where were they when I needed a care, maybe they were wearing their blinkers too, for in these day, and these times, that's what people do-

I know I am asking of something you may see wrong so why bother, but they're really a nice gift from the Corporation father, so father can I keep them, these blinkers work great as I will focus solely on my own faith.

The Answer: "The Good Samaritan" (Selfless)

Oh my little son how soon we forget, the teachings and the blessing you have been born with, for there once was a man a lawyer in fact, who tried to test my Son the same, way back. During the days of my beloved Son who was sent as payment for your sins, blinkers were in style also back then, as the lawyer wore his with pride speaking the truth he tried to test the truth as he asked my Son the light, 'What shall I do to receive eternal life', and without strife, for my Son already knew his deepest thoughts, simply replied, 'What is the law?' Surely he knew the lawyer deeds as he rephrased the question and asked, 'How does it read?' The lawyer replied without his pride for in this moment there was a change in tides and along with the tides went his pride, for what he said showed he was fed his daily bread from the living word and clearly he had heard the truth which explained clearly what you should do, and for a moment he dropped his façade and said, 'You shall love the Lord your God with all your heart and soul,' just as the bible told, 'with all your strength and all your mind,' we should love the lord till the end of time, 'also your neighbour as yourself,' explaining true love for everyone else. Jesus responded with, 'You have answered correctly do this and you should live,' for eternal life is of the Father to give, but then once again, 'Who is my neighbour?' the lawyer replied, unfortunately my Son would not be tried. My Son began to tell a tale, a tale that most know well, a story that will survive the ages of time one that would put to rest the lawyer's trying mind.

"A certain man going down from Jerusalem to Jericho" was beat down by some robbers, from head to toe they beat him and stripped him and left him to die, as he lay on the kerb while others passed him by-

First came a priest who could have at least lent a hand, but instead crossed the road when he saw the man, next came the Levite upon the same sight, with his blinkers intact he wouldn't do right, "he looked at the

man and passed by on the other side" neither man cared if he lived or died-

But then came "a Samaritan, travelling along" felt pity in his heart and knew it would be wrong, to pass another in such a moment of need, as he hurt and bled the Samaritan performed his deeds, "and bound up his wounds, pouring on them oil and wine" what love and compassion which is so hard to find-

When he was done he helped the man up upon his own beast, as the sun begun its journey to the east, he carried him to the nearest inn as he treated this stranger like his closest friend, paying the fee of his stay for that day to the keeper of the inn, and as he left the next day he would say, 'Take care of him, and whatever you spend I will pay you when I return,' as he continued to show his concern-

To check to see if the lawyer had learned, my Son asked of the three which do you think proved to be a good neighbour to the man in need? 'The man who took pity on him,' the lawyer replied knowing if he had passed him he would have died, and feeling he is well trained Jesus said, 'Then go and do the same.'

Because of God's grace to me, I have laid the foundation like an expert builder. Now others are building on it. But whoever is building on this foundation must be very careful. For no one can lay any foundation other than the one already laid, which is Jesus Christ.

Jesus Christ
"Where Is The Justice?"

Is it here, or is it there, sometimes I feel it's everywhere while at the same time existing nowhere, without a care for the law, serving itself raw, transcending logic, a borderline tragic, more elusive than magic, but forever held captive-

When in the presence of crime, forever she's blind, the all-seeing being, a most powerful queen and undeniable missing, at least it seems, but cannot be for to be without will spawn doubt, and all doubt creates, a lack of trust, but why must we trust when trust itself indicates, a shortage of honesty, and complicates to a certain degree, the very thing it must achieve-

Represented by the scale, who's telling the tale, but mostly fail, at filling the jails not with the guilty but instead the just, which means it can happen to any of us, at anytime, we can be found guilty as charged, and why I ask is this so hard to believe, that some remain free of the deed, committing a crime, and not serving their time-

To all it's known, of them high on their throne, judging others for crimes, when they have committed their own, how can it be, that we can be judged by someone more morally flawed, then all who appear when their names are called, standing before them and cases they hear, resulting in some serving many years for crimes they did not commit, all because of a fool who sits up high and his very existence is forged of a lie, for the truth is not found under the black gown, which conceals, and hides their evils within, but with a thump of their gavel your case begins-

Order in the court, oh me, oh my, and your very life hangs on an alibi, one with an incentive to set you free, another motivated to prove you guilty, nine sit and wait to decide your fate, while the one whose called judge contemplates, who is more believable of the two sides, and very life hinges on the case they've tried, for their victory results in who lives or dies, who's jailed or freed, in a system that's susceptible to distrust and greed, outside influence resulting in another life being ruined. If I ever had a question it would be just this, can someone please tell me, "Where is the Justice?"

How Would it be "To See No Love?"

A world without, love I doubt can last or survive, like an incapable hive failing to produce honey, a bank with no money, incapable of filling your withdrawal requests at best an empty space in one's chest, missing their heart, not able to feel remorse or sorrow, with no hope for tomorrow-

Feeling disconnected, highly neglected, all alone at home, with no food to eat, a song with no beat incapable of producing a melody or harmony, corrupt and unsmooth lacking a groove, just a shallow noise and nothing to move to-

The absence of compassion, a multitude of hate, food without taste, and time becomes timeless, as fear becomes boundless, at best you'll be killed at worse you will kill but still unable to be filled and satisfied by the kill, and at will you will kill and kill and kill again, until you find you have killed your family and friends-

In the end you'll wonder when did it come to be such a day, how could the world have come to such a place in

time, for our minds will fail to produce thoughts, defaulting on debts that had been bought by the blood of the Son as we contemplate what have we done-

As we are drowning in our tears, manifesting our fears as weeks becomes months and months becomes years, now turning to God to get out of here, as he will ask, who are you, I know not of you, for the spirit is truth and you were untrue so there's nothing in heaven for either of you and in that moment the father will ask, what do you speak of for wasn't it you who could see no love?

Is It Okay to Choose Who We Love?

Even now if I was to ask whom do you love what would you say or what will you think of? Would whatever you say be the truth, or would it merely be the truth to you? Would you truly believe the answer you give or at that very moment will you feel, the hate for your enemies begin racing through your mind as if your inner spirit tries to find the secret you've buried deep within as you hated your enemies but loved your friends-

See you may be able to lie in the flesh but there are no lies in the spirit, only the test, so before you even bother remember your spirit is not yours but belongs to the Father. So I would ask you again whom do you love my friend and if your answer is short of everyone then you need to start remembering the example of Jesus the Son, and start taking the steps to bring your personal beliefs into reconciliation with your personal beef-

Blurring, fading and then morphing the two into one, just as both feel the warmth of the sun, receive shelter from the rain, you should love your friends and enemies all the same. For love is our source of connectivity to one another and no matter the births from different mothers, under the Father we're all sisters and brothers forever connected and bonded to one another-

As he commanded, we are required to love one and all until the day our names are called. For that day before the father we'll stand, every child, every woman, and every man, as he reads our name from the Book of Life, revealing it all, every wrong and every right and if you were the one who saw no love, then you too will not be seen by the our Father above.

"Whoever does not love does not know God, because God is love." (1 John 4:8)

A Gift for You My Friend "A Set of Blinkers"

For you I bring a gift... to have, to hold and do what you will with, they're yours for life, sure to cause pain and strife, with your co-workers and friends, breaking down relationships from within, you have never seen a gift so grand, alleviating the need for taking a stand, you can just focus ahead, and move along, blocking it out until it's gone, for the darkness that's upon you will surely pass, for it always does and never lasts-

These blinkers my friends are great, providing you focus, and keeping you straight, with the ability to see only the right, and ignoring the wrong, for why fight at work when you can fight at home? Why donate to the needy when you can get ahead by giving to the greedy, why should you care when the art of true caring is so rare, never mind whose home was lost in the flood, was it yours all covered in mud?-

Hurricanes, tornadoes, or even forest fires, you've experienced none so why not enjoy all your desires, why should you be sad or mad or even feel bad, when you've lost nothing and still wearing the latest fad-

They had a chance to get a job, was it by you they've been rob... No... and shame on those who make us feel low, you can thank God, and work real hard and they still make you feel bad about the cards you've been dealt claiming you don't understand for you've never felt the suffering of losing your land, their sorrow, their pain and bad health, as they're eroded due to the death of their family and friends whose lives came to a tragic end-

I tell you my friend with these blinkers your suffering will end, straight ahead you'll see, in your own little world you will be, just look at me, just as happy as one can be. I smile every day and by night I pray, thanking the Lord that I'm okay, thanking the Lord for all I received, and hoping in me he is pleased, and I am certain my words were heard by God, because I'm a good person who works real hard, I don't make trouble for others as I live like the boy in the plastic bubble-

Well, enough said for what else can I say, they are yours to wear every single day, the more you wear them, the more you'll like them, and someday you will forget all about them, as they will become a part of your life, that which you can share with your husband or wife. It may start off as an opinion or even advice, but give it time to dampen the light, and before you know, you'll be good to go, going with the flow, morphing to become a part of the status quo-

For you my friend I give this gift to have and to hold to do what you will with, but just remember in the end, we will all be held accountable for our sins.

If There Ever Was a Gift to Reject

If there ever was a gift to reject, I would be remiss or even regret if I failed to say those blinkers are it, for like a cold and flu one sneeze can send it from me to you, and from you to him, and he to them, and then to all of the physical realm-

What would be left is a world without love, and life without passion, as tears will fall from above, as the angels cry for the loss of compassion. The art of true caring will be lost, and what a shame for have we forgotten the cost? How could we forget the price that was paid, the sacrifices made, for the foundation to be laid, the cross that was carried, the man that was buried, the only man to ever see God, who healed, and taught from his heart-

Have we forgotten the cost to the Father, and why he bothered to deliver his Son in the hands of the ones who mocked him, flogged him, blindfolded and struck him as they continued to insult him and alongside two robbers they murdered him, and even as he suffered and died, he could still show mercy to one of the robbers to his side, for the robber's defence of Christ, Jesus replied, 'This very day you will be with me in paradise' never once wearing blinkers as would me or you, he still showed love that was ever so true, saying, 'Father, forgive them, for they know not what they do'-

So to you I say this very day although you may think it's okay, to accept this gift made for rejection, accepting it could cause your neglection, your lost reflection, in the eyes of perfection, no longer connected you'll lose your protection. You will fall victim to your enemies, and even as you pray on your knees, your words would be as a small boat crossing rough seas, a single leaf in the Fall in a forest of trees, a single buzzing sound in a hive of bees, for all of your words would be lost and unheard-

For all those suffering in pain, and crying in the rain, homes and lives that were lost at unbelievable cost, all those who felt hungry but could not eat, unable to survive for being too weak, those that fell victim to the hurricane and earthquake, shivering in fear, searching for a break, those who floated away in the floods, with homes covered in mud, those who lost their jobs or have been slain as they got robbed, would have been Christ coming into your life-

As he arrived on your left and right, give thanks to your blinkers as he was kept from your sight, as you were focussed straight ahead instead of on the words he said, and now having doubts as you realize you've missed out, so if there ever was a gift meant to reject, for that case blinkers are perfect, for in this case and in this time, you will find that blinkers only aid in manipulating your mind.

Father Where Are You, I Can't See You

Our Father who are in heaven where are you for I cannot see you, you were my light and truth, now what shall I do, where I once felt protected I now feel rejected. Could it be as a result from wearing my blinkers, as I receded from the world of all the thinkers, for all the times I pretended not to see those who were in need, those I saw bleed, those I let starve and thirst, as I put my own comforts first, those I left crying and dying, hoping I would return only to learn I was lying-

If only I had known or been shown the path on which so few have travelled that which is made of light and not that of gravel, if only I had a map to guide my way, I would not have ended up in this place this day. Oh Lord can you not feel my pain, as I'm going insane, sure I feel some guilt but I played the hand that I had been dealt and though I took the wide path travelled by many, I performed some good deeds though not plenty it was a few so what can I do-

Can I pray today, in a special place in a special way, to get you once again to hear what I say, can I do your work, that one day out of the week, and if I am slapped again now turn the other cheek? I am begging you for I don't care to reap, what I've sown for I've known for so long that this day would come, to account for my wrong, but now that it's here I fear, for I thought there would be more time for me, to make up for my wrong, but where has the time gone, for my life flew by as I missed the signs for I had not a clue... okay maybe that's not true, for I knew of the Saviour sent by you, but my blinkers keep me focussed on myself, how could I be expected to see someone else-

Please Father hear my cry, see my pain, give me shelter from the freezing rain, bring me in from out of the storm, let me find peace in your home, Father where are you, I can't see you, I feel afraid as if all alone in a deep dark cave, as I try to find your Son in order to be saved. Straight ahead is all I can see, not left nor right nor to the back of me so, if you can, please show yourself to my front, I promise you I would run-

Oh my God, oh Lord, please, please, please I'm down on my knees have you no pity to show for me, I feel so lost and can't be found, as my darkness stretches from the heavens to the ground. I'm scared, oh God, what do I do, terrorized by the truth, Father where are you; for my light is lost, I can't see you.

Father Please Help Me to Take Them Off

Fear not for all is not lost, for our Father in Heaven has paid the cost, and the price was high and steep, as he paid with blood his Son spilled in the streets. Giving us the chance to be forgiven and saved, as long as we learn to correct our ways-

So in secret kneel to him and pray and in case you are wondering what to say, Jesus himself was very aware which is why he delivered to us this prayer-

"Our Father which are in heaven, Hallowed be your name. Your Kingdom come, your will be done in Earth, as it is in Heaven. Give us this day our daily bread, and forgive us our debts, as we forgive our debtors. And lead us not into temptation, but deliver us from evil: For yours are the kingdom, and the power, and the glory, forever. Amen."

Please don't mistake the simplicity of this short, but mighty, group of words of beauty, forming this prayer for it is plenty, "for the Father knows what you need before you ask him". Still never forget the two great commandments, for they will be remembered during your judgment, for Jesus said, 'The Lord our God is one Lord; and you shall love the Lord your God with your whole heart, with your whole soul, with your whole mind and with your whole strength,' as he is ensuring we all are on the same wavelength-

Don't stop there for there is something else "You shall love your neighbour as yourself. There are no greater commandments than these" so please remember these words you have heard for they are of the Son and they are one in agreement with each other for to truly love is to love one another. So to remove your blinkers "Give to the one who asks you, and do not turn away from the one who wants to borrow from you" for these are not only the deeds of a heart that is true but also the commandments the Lord sent to you-

When all else fails and you're feeling cruel, just always remember the golden rule, which is to do unto others as you would wish they do unto you.

"Will there ever be True Justice"

The day will come, for one and for all, where the living and the dead names will be called; we'll stand as he reads from the Book of Life, for he is the true knower of whose naughty or nice-

All the secrets are known, all the bones will be shown, that which was hidden in the dark, will be brought to the light, bringing shame to all who's in his sight, he'll be perfect in every way, as he reads your work of all your days, every second, minute, and hour, will be seen, every thought, every feeling, and every dream, so to you beware, forif you dare, take a chance for this Judge will not be a man-

Listen close to my words my friend, for your time to speak would have come to an end, so the time is now to correct your ways, it's time to pray, for forgiveness now before the last day, for when it comes it will be swift, so look at his mercy now as a gift, and accept it now with all your heart, and keep his teaching when the time becomes hard, for the world as you know it will come to an end so accept Jesus now for it will be too late then, for the end is the end and the Judge will judge-

The Justice will be just, so if you must, repent in your ways, meditate and pray, for the Judge himself will be the truth, the Justice also true in fact the purest form of truth for this moment of truth will be the living truth-

"And the Word was made flesh, and dwelt among us, (and we beheld his glory, the glory as of the only begotten of the Father,) full of grace and truth." (John 1:14)

"The Spirit gives life; the flesh counts for nothing. The words I have spoken to you are spirit and they are life." (John 6:63)

"What Is the Corporation?"

The Corporation is the name I have given to explain the body of individuals that will come together from many different nations, religions and ideological backgrounds to form a single body with the intentions of governing not only the world but the entire Universe. They are derivative of countless religions and beliefs, from all walks of life, neither from here nor there but of everywhere. They have dissected all aspects of the world's histories and religions, past and present, calculated the cause and effects, analyzed all the risks which are accepted and not accepted. They have learned and recognized the skill with which the Creators have created their greatest works through chaos, and have started to use this technique on all of us to re-create our very existence. Even the Father's most precious creation, man himself, is born out of chaos, for from the chaos of birth is born man in their very image. The Corporation realized if the Creators can create their great masterpieces out of chaos, then that must be the secret and missing equation from their well calculated formula. They realized that the "Theory of Relativity" is real and that all beings that were brought into existence by the Creators are all dependent on the other.

Furthermore, they realized their "New World Order" is not just a change but a re-creation. They realize, if they are going to re-create our very existence, they must be perfect in quality, perfect in nature and, most important, perfect in completeness, evading all limits to restrictions and exceptions. There must be no conditions, and the plan must be final, since they would have to leave the "Body of Christ" being disconnected from the whole. This decision must be finite because once they leave the "Body of Christ" it would be written for all eternity resulting in their names being erased from the "Book of Life", only to be replaced with one common identity and to be known by this identity from the beginning of existence to the end of days.

The elite group created their "Grand Charter", recognizing it as a separate legal entity having its own rights, privileges and liabilities from those of the Creators' and all that they created. Now instead of being a part of the "Body of Christ" they are now the "Body of Corporate" created to govern or rule mankind. The "Word" refers to them as the "Antichrist".

"They went out from us, but they did not really belong to us. For if they had belonged to us, they would have remained with us; but their going showed that none of them belonged to us." (1 John 2:19)

ND - #0244 - 080726 - C14 - 197/132/20 - PB - 9781844268597 - Gloss Lamination